Time for PHONICS

1

Marion Ireland

READING BEGINS
WITH INITIAL SOUNDS

Hunter Education Nightingale

HUNTER
EDUCATION
NIGHTINGALE

Time for Phonics Book 1

Published by:
Hunter Education Nightingale
ABN: 69 055 798 626
PO Box 547
Warners Bay NSW 2282
Ph: 0417 658 777
email: sales@huntereducationnightingale.com.au
paul@huntereducationnightingale.com.au
www.huntereducationnightingale.com.au

Cover Design: Brooke Lewis

National Library of Australia Card No.
and ISBN 978 - 1 - 925787 - 04 - 7
Phonics Series ISBN 978 - 1 - 925787 - 08 - 5

RECYCLING

When the program is completed and the paper no longer wanted, be sure to have it recycled. The time and care taken to recycle may help save a tree and maintain our environment.

E D C B A
22 21 20 19 18

Time for Phonics

Initial Sounds

About this Book

- This book is based on initial sounds of the letters in the alphabet as shown.
- It includes speech rhymes and phonic jingles to help children to clearly articulate each sound. Teachers need to check the correct position of lips, tongue, teeth.
- Student activity pages incorporating oral, aural, visual and kinaesthetic strategies - a multi sensory approach.
- Assessment tasks at regular intervals.
- Final Assessment Task covering letter sound/relationships a - z and related activities including reading and writing CVC words.

Each double page follows the same pattern as the one shown for **s**:

- Speech rhyme - **s** sound
- Trace and colour upper and lower case letter shapes
- Phonic jingle - **s** sound
- Phonemic awareness - identify and colour pictures with the same initial **s** sound
- Use picture clues to read words with the initial **s** sound.
- Assessment tasks include children writing one missing letter (initial, middle, end) as part of CVC word/picture matching plus creating some CVC words themselves using known single sounds.

Letter/sound relationships taught in this order:

s m c t a b f g - assessment task

r i n e d h o l - assessment task

p w k j qu v x y z - assessment task

Final assessment tasks can be used for reporting and diagnostic purposes.

Message to Teacher and Parents

- A child's first year at school is vital.
- Strong foundations are needed to ensure future progress in all aspects of literacy.
- Reading to children is an essential part of every child's literacy journey.
- Rhymes and repetition, phonic jingles and stories all play an important part, helping children to embrace literacy learning.
- Note the position of lips, tongue and teeth to ensure correct articulation of each initial sound. Mirrors can be helpful!
- Oral practice needs to precede all written tasks.
- Developing phonemic awareness is part of the process.
- Learning letter/sound relationships provides a basis for formal reading.
- Applying letter/sound relationships to form words by running the sounds together is a tried and proven teaching method.
- Learning to trace and copy each letter shape is also an important part of the process.
- Provide lots of encouragement and praise for effort.

Message to Students

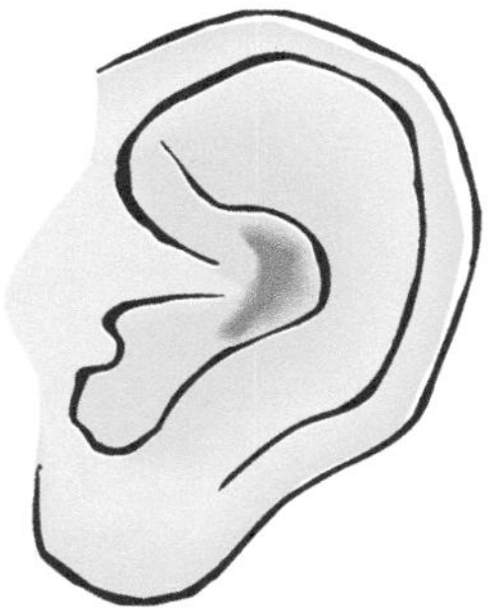

Listen to the sounds

Look at the letter shape

Think

Speak clearly

Write letter shapes neatly

Sammy Snail

Practise saying the speech rhyme about *s*.

Little Sammy Snail
Is very, very slow,
But he slithers up to Sally
As fast as he can go.

Track the letter *s* between the lines. Start at the red dot.

Track

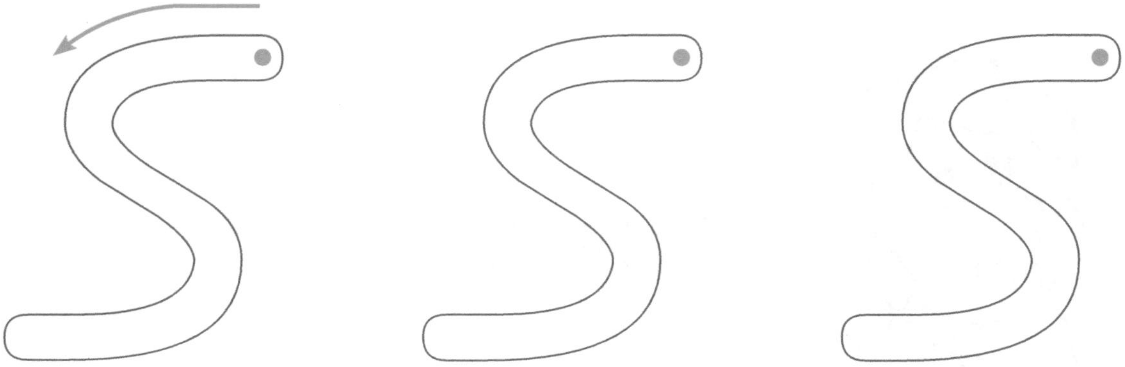

Trace the letter *s*. Start at the red dot.

Trace

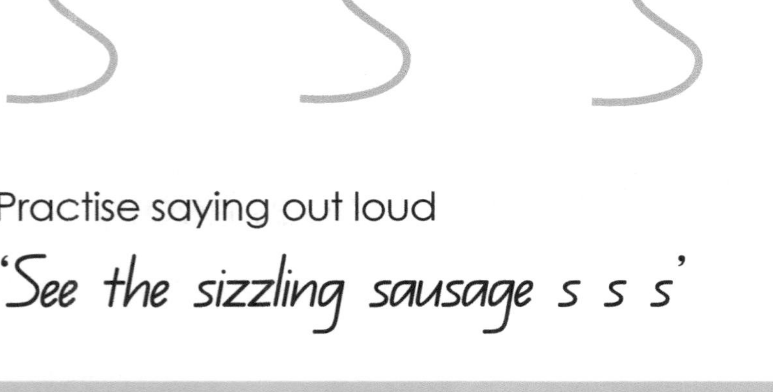

Practise saying out loud

'See the sizzling sausage s s s'

Colour the pictures in the row that begin with *s* sound.

 snail	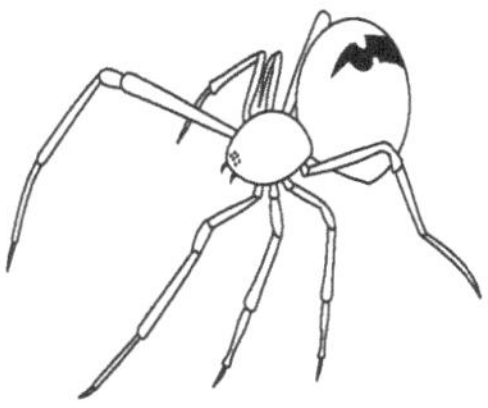 spider	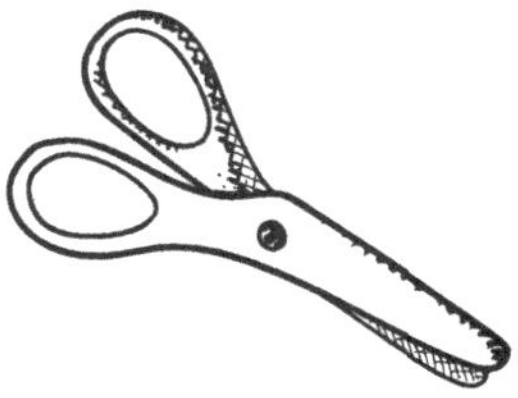 scissors	 doll
 sun	 pony	 sock	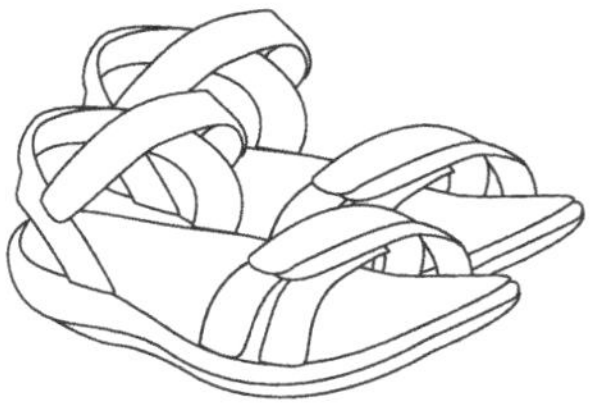 sandal
 star	 snake	 dog	 swan
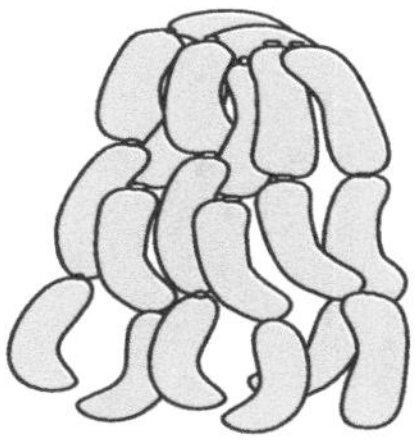 sausages	 cat	 six	 santa

Use the picture clues to read these words starting with *s*.

 six	 sun	 sock	 snail

The Man in the Moon

Practise saying the speech rhyme about *m*.

The man in the moon
Met a monkey from Mars,
They drank Milky Way milk
And looked at the stars.

Track the letter *M* between the lines. Start at the red dot.

Track

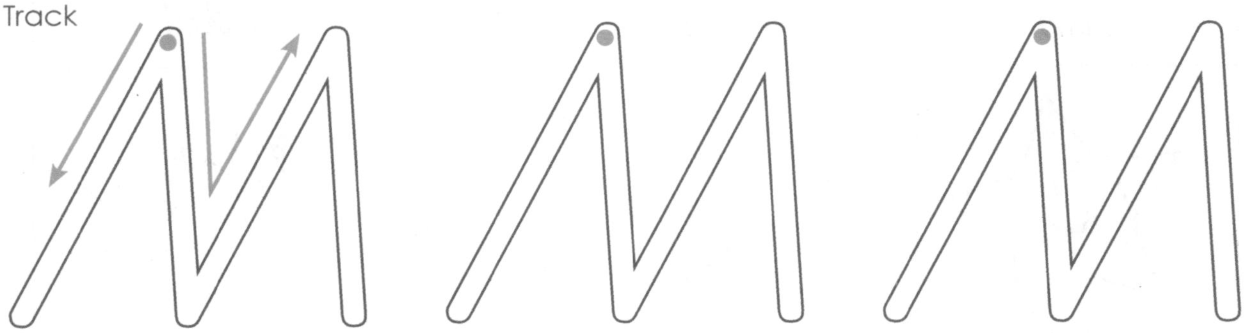

Trace the letter *m*. Start at the red dot.

Trace

Practise saying out loud

'mumbling monkeys m m m'

Colour the pictures in the row that begin with *m* sound.

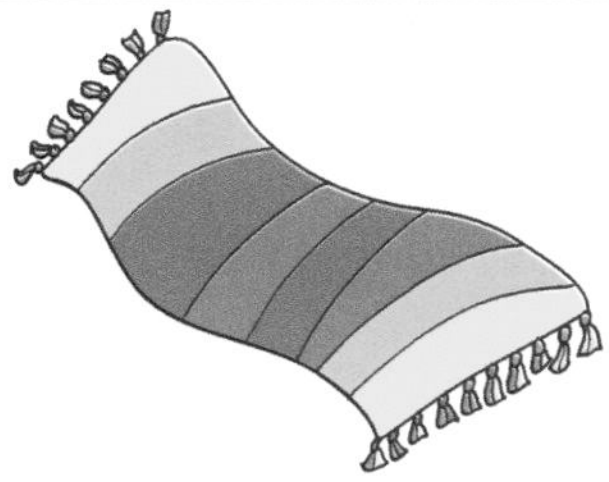 mat	 baby	 mobile phone	 money
 mop	 mug	 milk	 snail
 moon	 mouse	 cat	 marbles
 monkey	 mud	 map	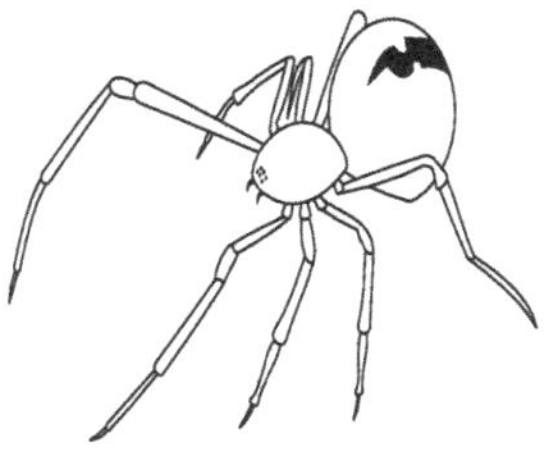 spider

Use the picture clues to read these words starting with *m*.

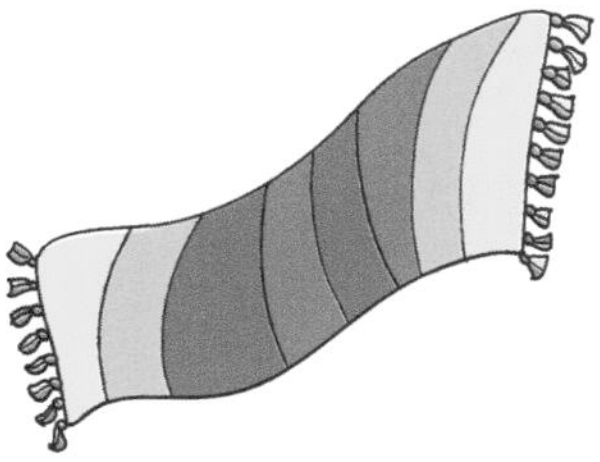			
mat	mop	moon	monkey

Caterpillar

Practise saying the speech rhyme about *c*.

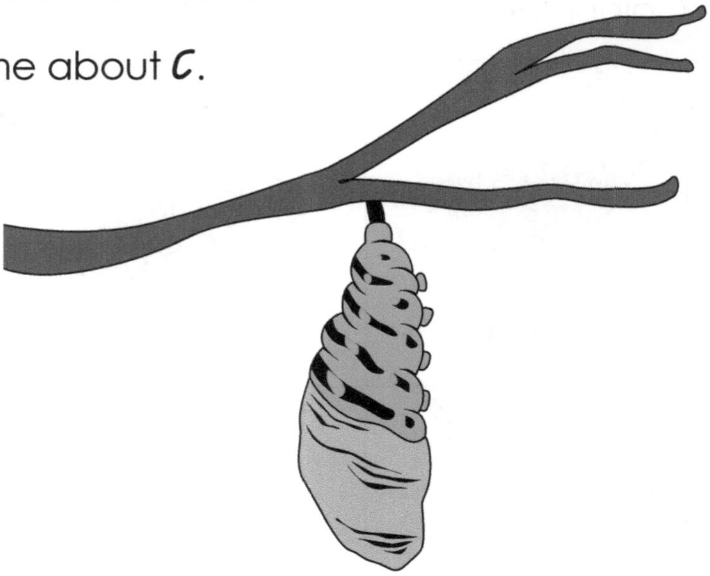

Caterpillar, caterpillar,
In a cocoon,
Can I see a butterfly
Coming out soon?

Track the letter *C* between the lines. Start at the red dot.

Track

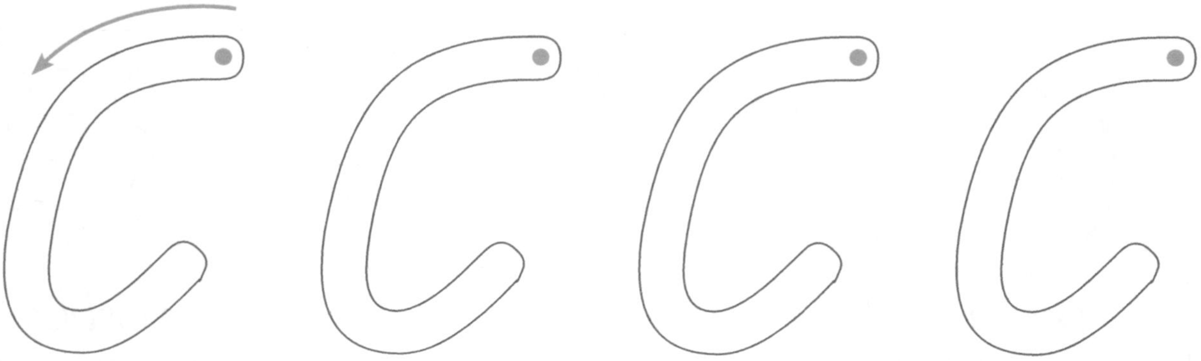

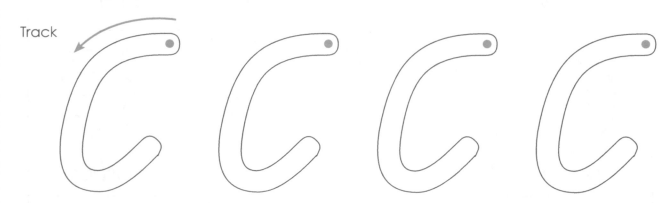

Trace the letter *c*. Start at the red dot.

Trace

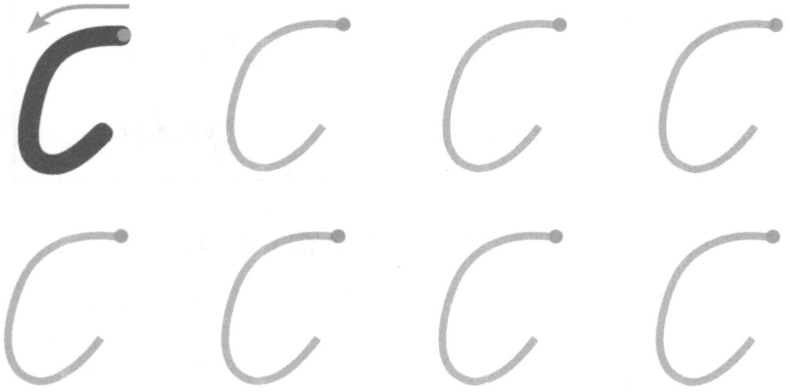

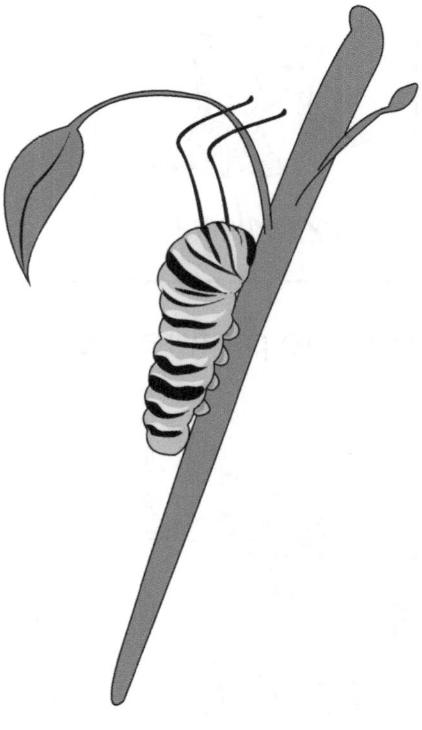

Practise saying out loud

'caterpillar climbing c c c'

Colour the pictures in the row that begin with *c* sound.

 cat	 cupcake	 candy cane	 mouse
 cup	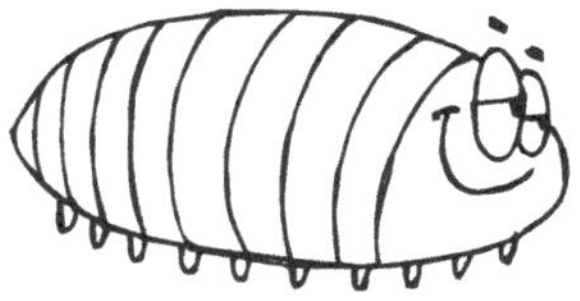 caterpillar	 castle	 crown
 cot	 moon	 carrot	 camera
 crab	 car	 cow	 calf

Use the picture clues to read these words starting with *c*.

cat

cup

cot

crab

Tim's Toy Train

Practise saying the speech rhyme about *t*.

Tickety tack,
Tickety tack,
The train's in a tunnel
Down the track.

Track the letter *T* between the lines. Start at the red dot.

Track

Trace the letter *t*. Start at the red dot.

Trace

Practise saying out loud

'tumbling tigers t t t'

Colour the pictures in the row that begin with *t* sound.

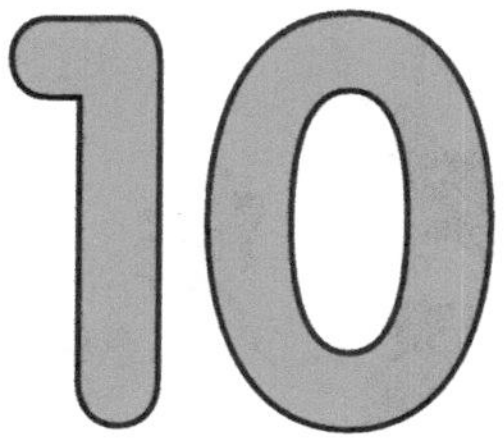 ten	 crab	 tree	 tortoise
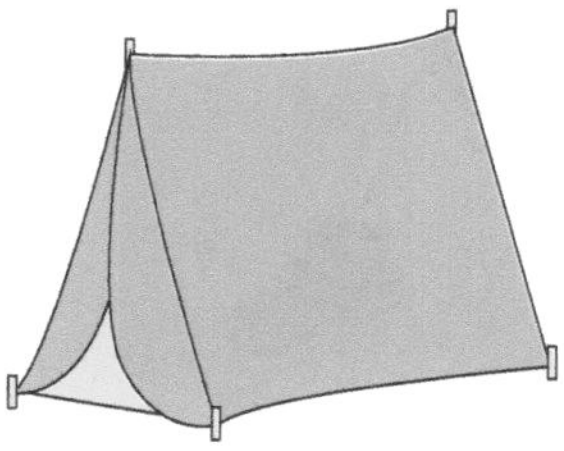 tent	 tiger	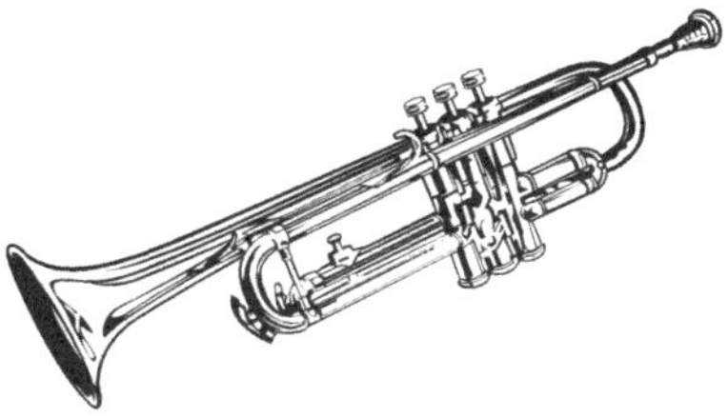 trumpet	 television
 tap	 moon	 torch	 truck
 train	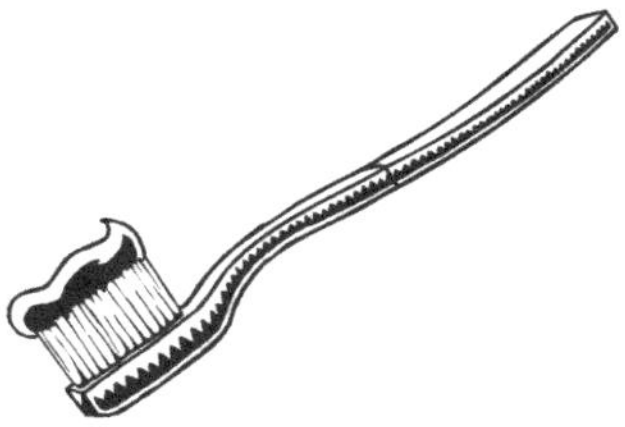 toothbrush	 torch	 crown

Use the picture clues to read these words starting with *t*.

ten

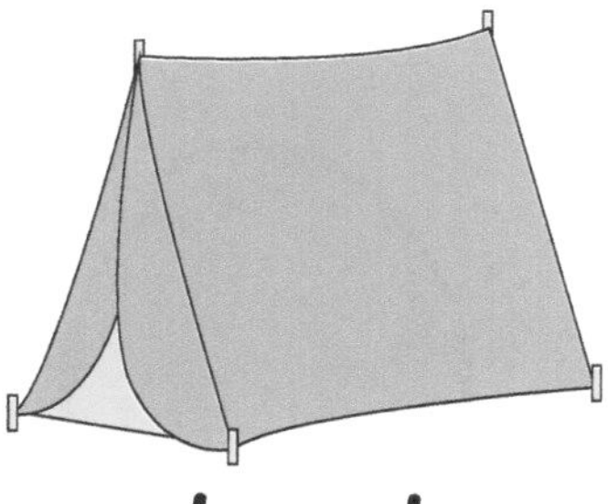
tent

tap

train

Ants

Practise saying the speech rhyme about *a*.

Ants in the attic,
Ants on my toe,
Ants on my ankle,
Go away, go!

Track the letter *A* between the lines. Start at the red dot.

Track

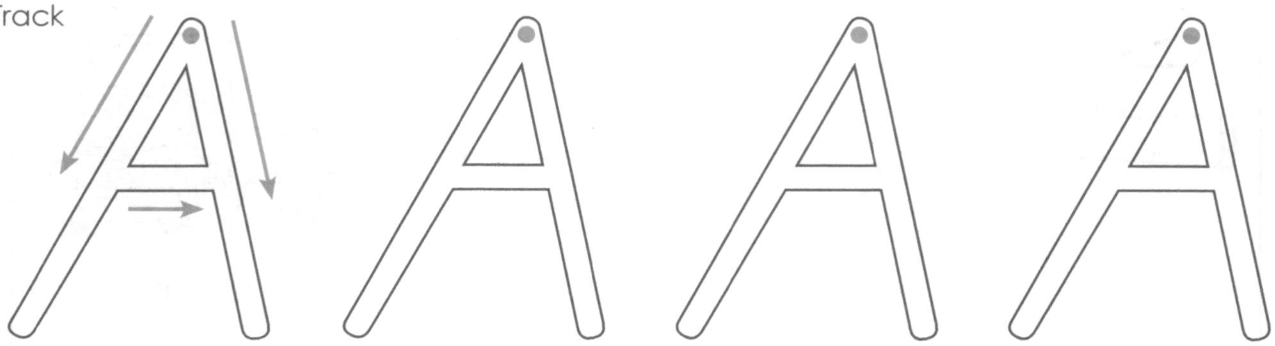

Trace the letter *a*. Start at the red dot.

Trace

Practise saying out loud

'Anna's apples a a a'

Colour the pictures in the row that begin with *a* sound.

 ant	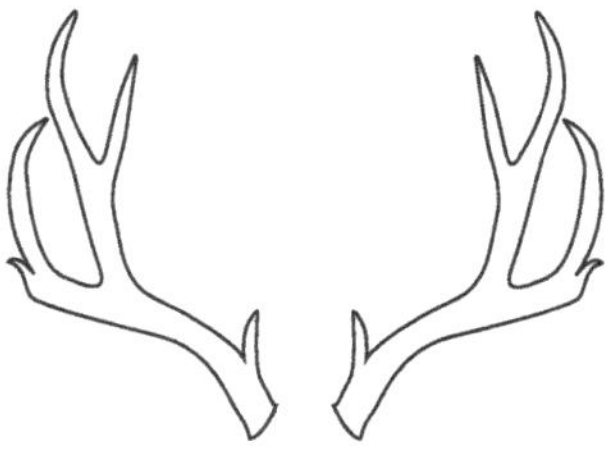 antlers	 star	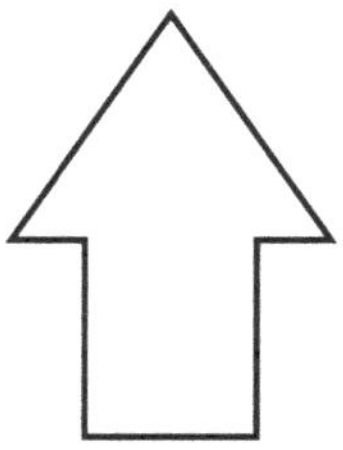 arrow
 apple	 anchor	 mug	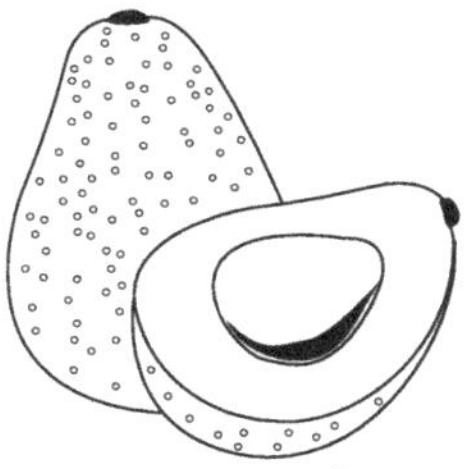 avocado
 axe	 ambulance	 butterfly	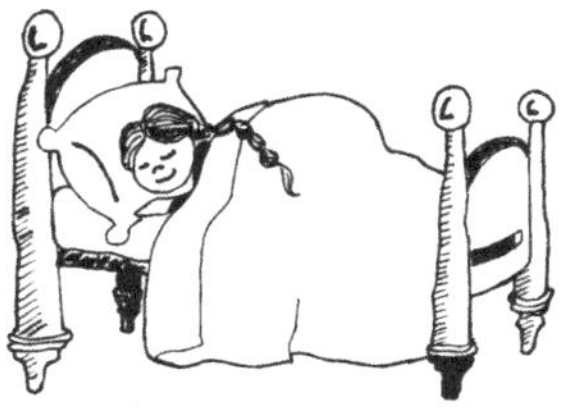 asleep
 astronaut	 alphabet	 train	 atlas

Use the picture clues to read these words starting with *a*.

ant apple axe astronaut

Blowing Bubbles

Practise saying the speech rhyme about *b*.

I blew a little bubble
I blew and could not stop,
My bubble just got bigger till
It burst with a great big POP!

Track the letter *B* between the lines. Start at the red dot.

Track

Trace the letter *b*. Start at the red dot.

Trace

Practise saying out loud

'bouncing balls b b b'

Colour the pictures in the row that begin with *b* sound.

 bat	 truck	 bike	 boat
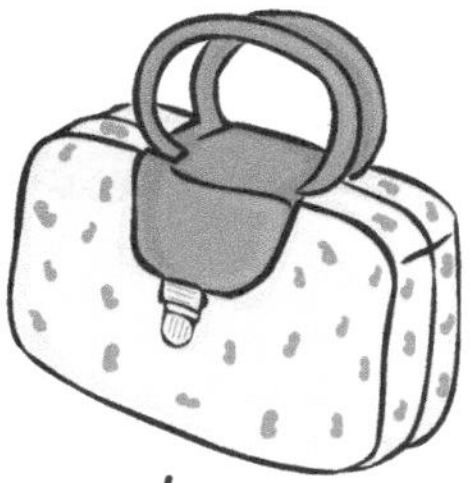 bag	 balloon	 boys	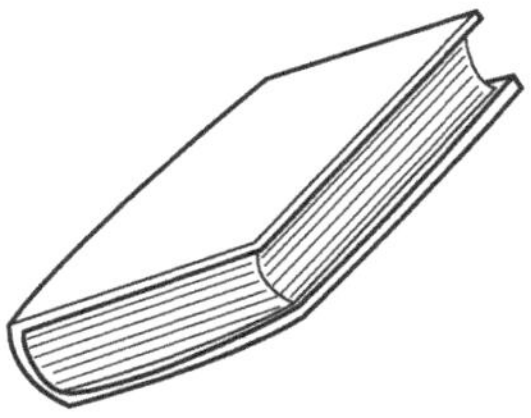 book
 bus	 ball	 baby	 bubble
 bed	 bird	 banana	 apple

Use the picture clues to read these words starting with *b*.

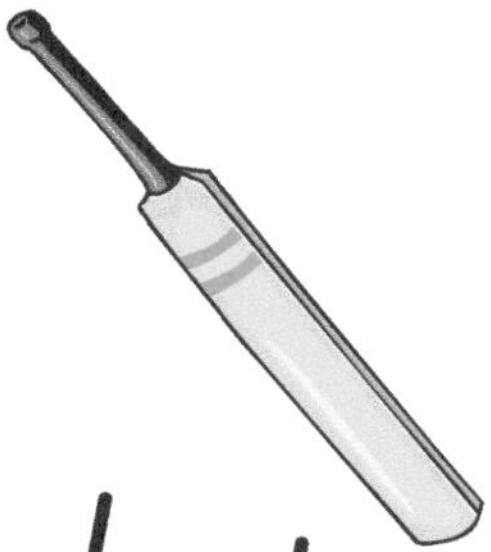
bat

bag

bed

bus

Five Fat Frogs

Practise saying the speech rhyme about *f*.

Five fat freckled frogs
sitting in the sun.
Five frogs' tongues went FLICK!
And five flies were gone.

Track the letter *F* between the lines. Start at the red dot.

Track

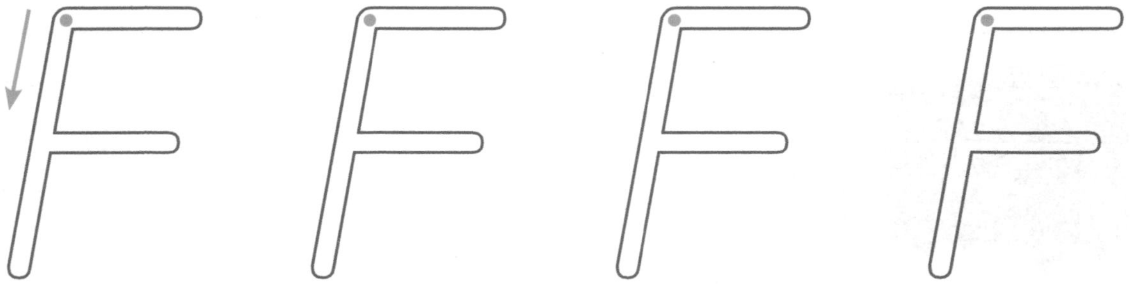

Trace the letter *f*. Start at the red dot.

Trace

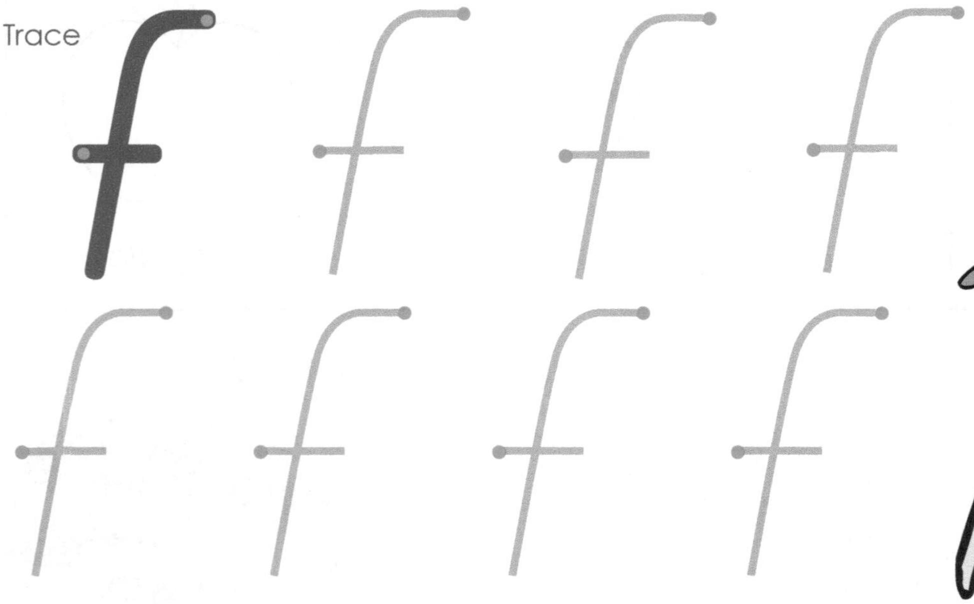

Practise saying out loud

'flippers flapping f f f'

Colour the pictures in the row that begin with *f* sound.

 fan	 ball	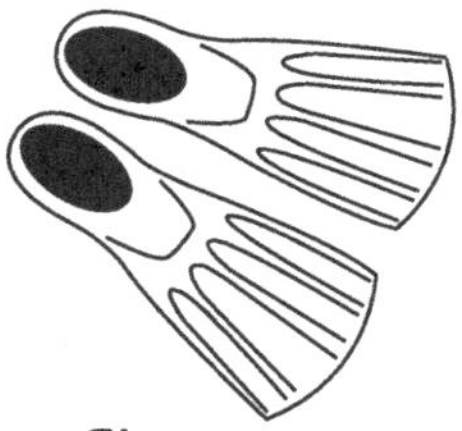 flippers	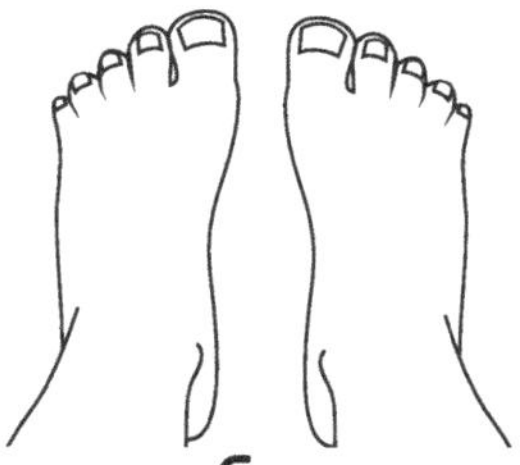 feet
 frog	 flower	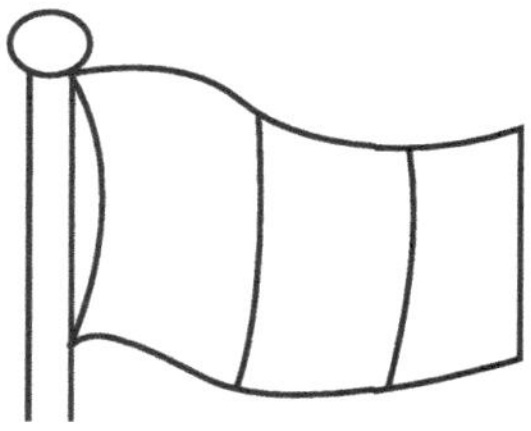 flag	 cow
4 four	 tent	 fire	 fork
5 five	 fish	 fly	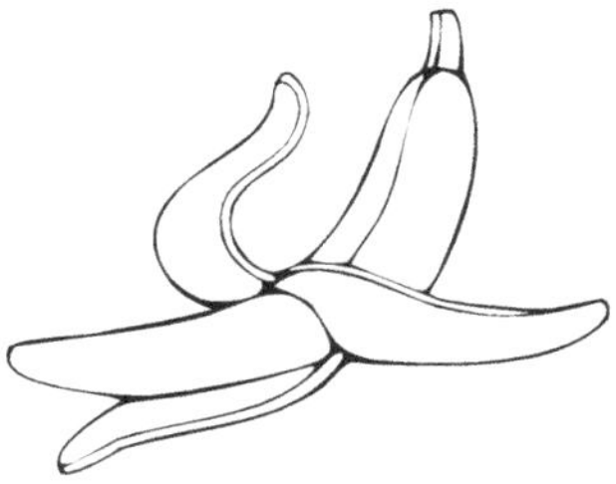 banana

Use the picture clues to read these words starting with *f*.

fan

frog

4
four

5
five

Gertrude Goat

Practise saying the speech rhyme about *g*.

Gertrude is a greedy goat
A greedy goat of mine –
She chews up Grandpa's gumboots
And clothes pegged on the line.

Track the letter *G* between the lines. Start at the red dot.

Track

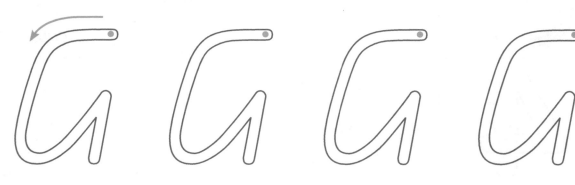

Trace the letter *g*. Start at the red dot.

Trace

Practise saying out loud

'giggling girls g g g'

Colour the pictures in the row that begin with g sound.

 grub	 grapes	 ghost	 tortoise
 grass	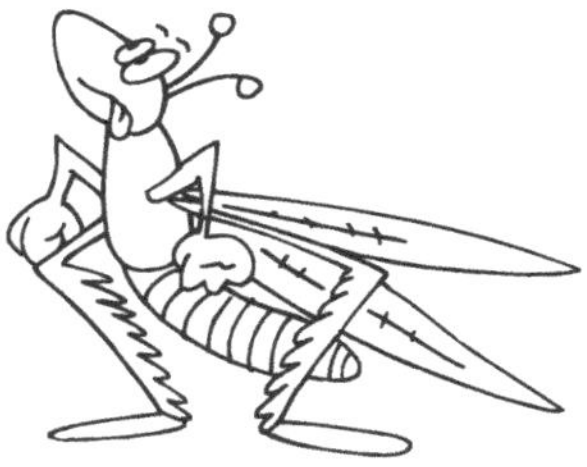 grasshopper	 marbles	 goose
 goat	 garden	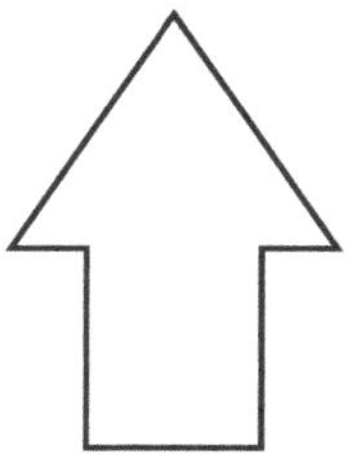 arrow	 guitar
 goldfish	 bike	 girl	 garage

Use the picture clues to read these words starting with g.

grub

grass

goat

giraffe

Beginning Sounds

Circle the letter that makes the beginning sound to match each picture.

t c m

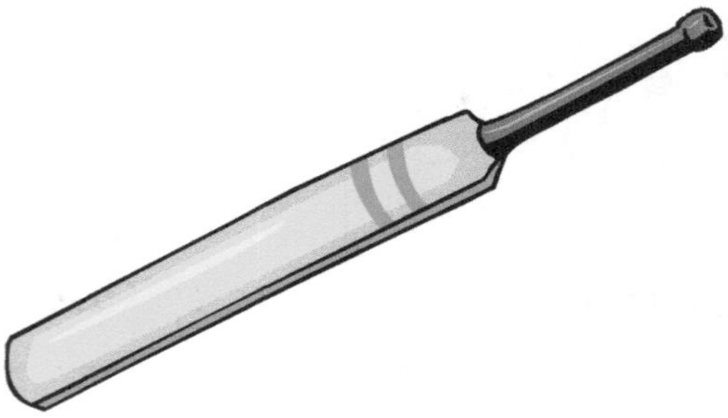

f a b

s t g

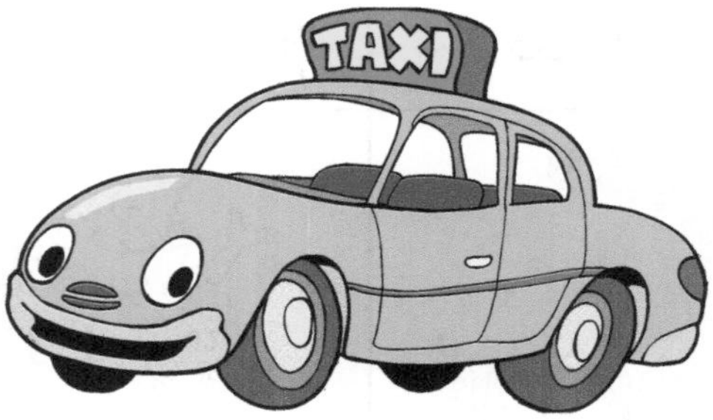

m c t

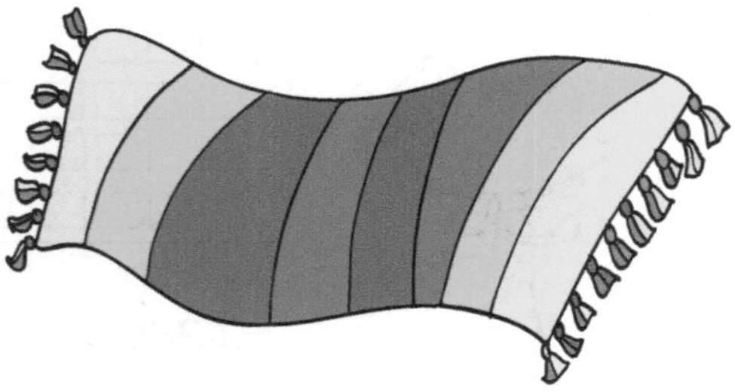

a f m

b g c

Read

a fat cat

Missing Letters

Write the missing letters.

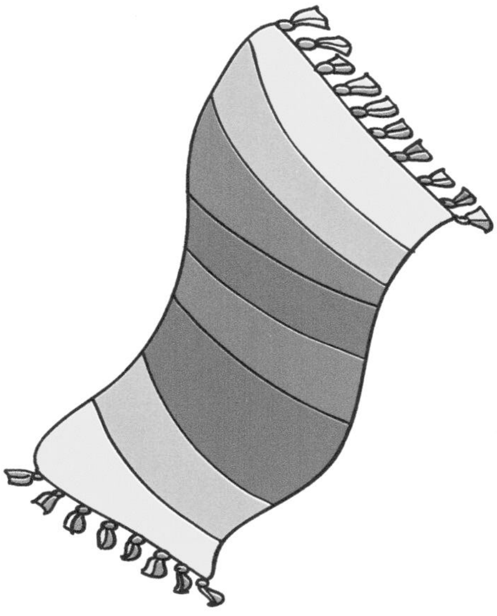
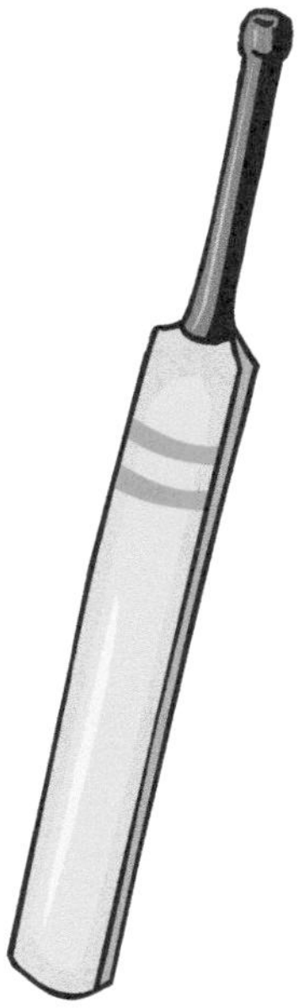

____ at   ____ at   ____ at

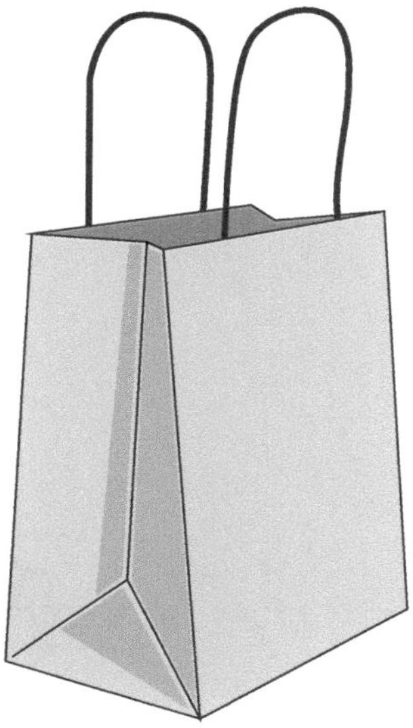
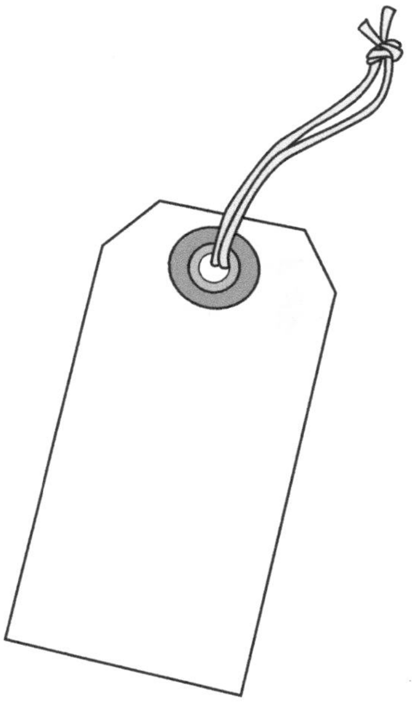

____ at   ____ ag   ____ ag

Running

Practise saying the speech rhyme about *r*.

Run to the rainbow,
Run to the sea,
Run to the mountains,
Run back to me!

Track the letter *R* between the lines. Start at the red dot.

Track

R R R R

Trace the letter *r*. Start at the red dot.

Trace

r r r
r r r

Practise saying out loud

'running racehorse r r r'

Colour the pictures in the row that begin with *r* sound.

 rat	 rain	 rainbow	 scissors
 ram	 rose	 rock	 map
 run	 camera	 ring	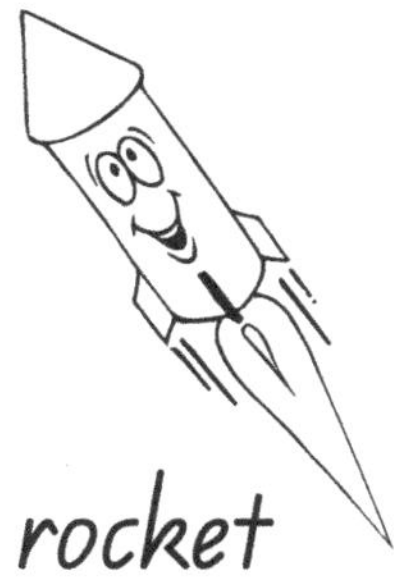 rocket
 rug	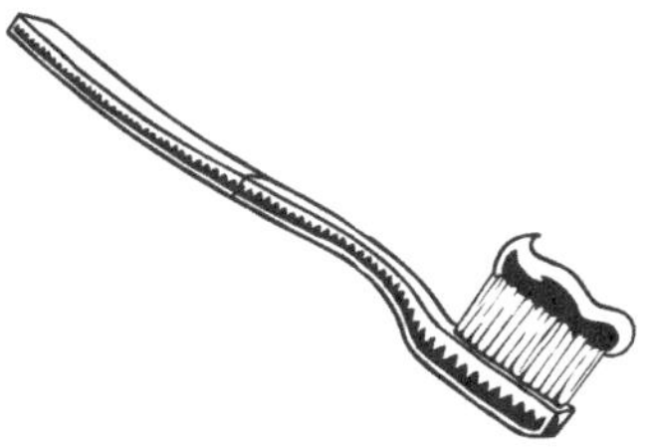 toothbrush	 rabbit	 rooster

Use the picture clues to read these words starting with *r*.

rat

ram

run

rug

Icky Icky Rubbish

Practise saying the speech rhyme about *i*.

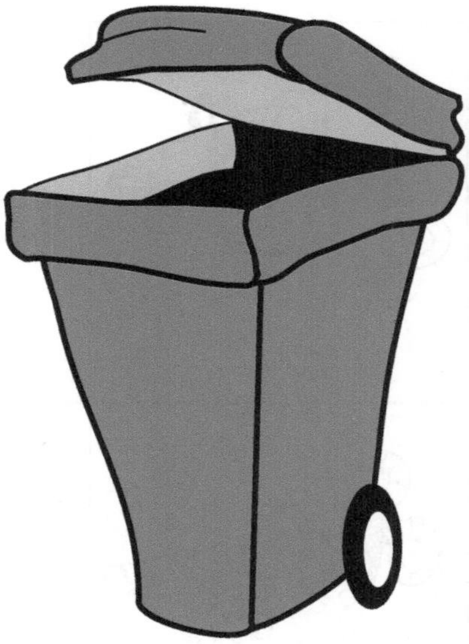

Icky icky rubbish,
Paper, scraps or tin.
If you see some rubbish,
Put it in the bin.

Track the letter *I* between the lines. Start at the red dot.

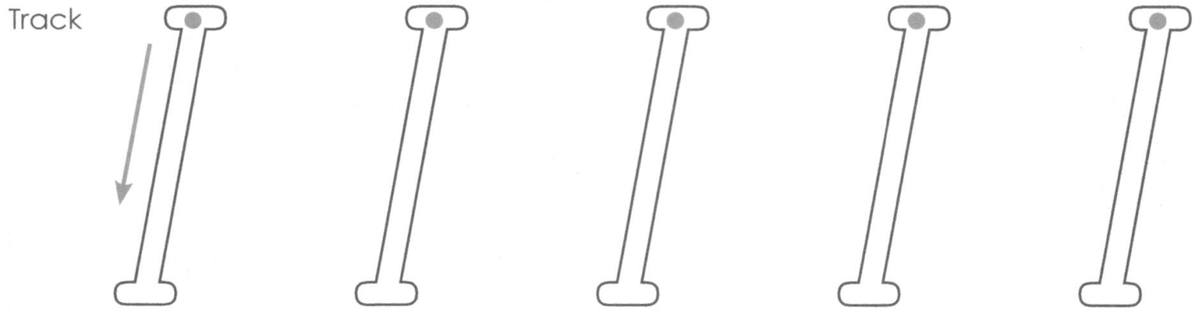

Trace the letter *i*. Start at the red dot.

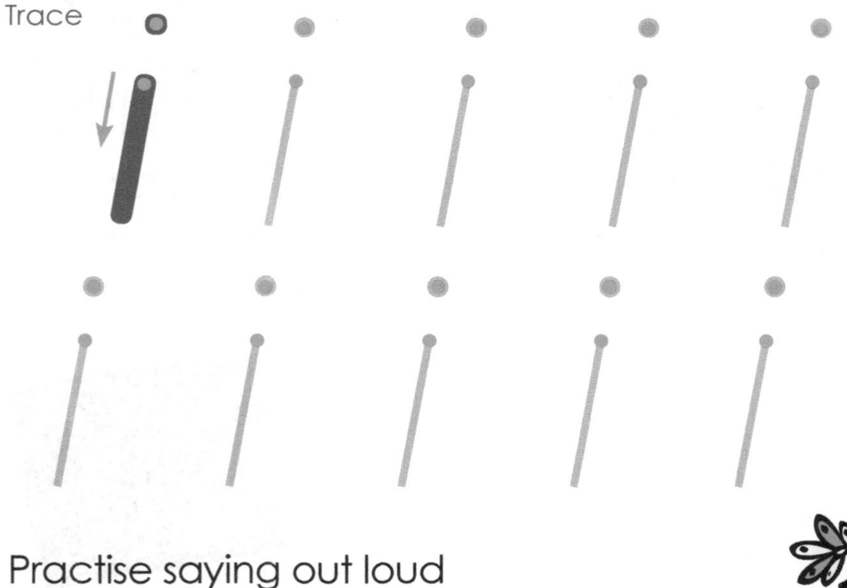

Practise saying out loud

'itchy indians i i i'

Colour the pictures in the row that begin with the short and long *i* sounds.

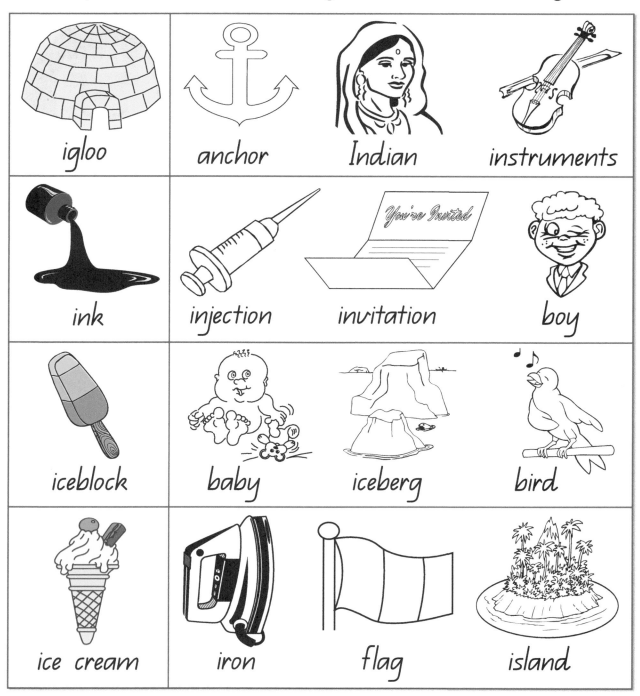

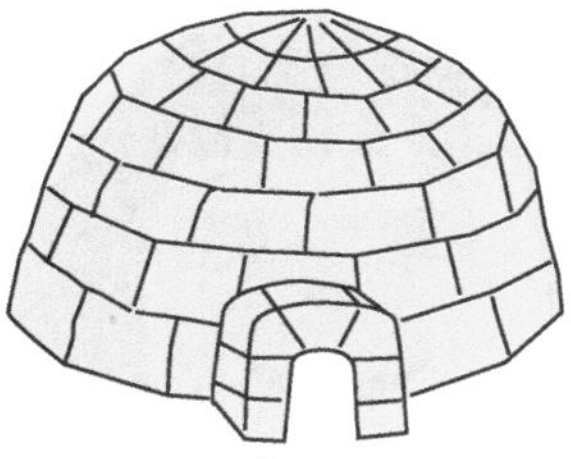 igloo	 anchor	 Indian	 instruments
 ink	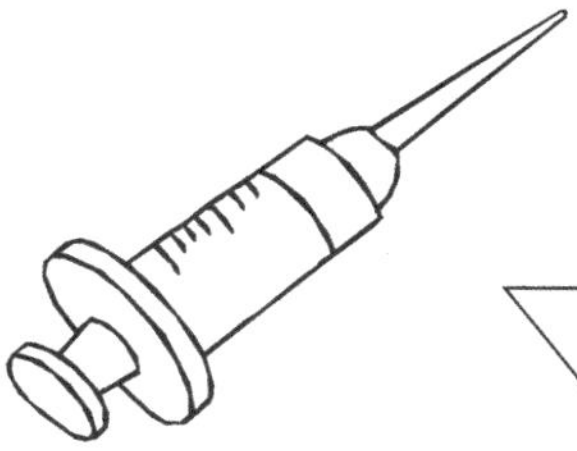 injection	 invitation	 boy
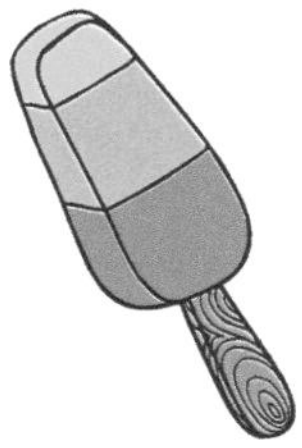 iceblock	 baby	 iceberg	 bird
 ice cream	 iron	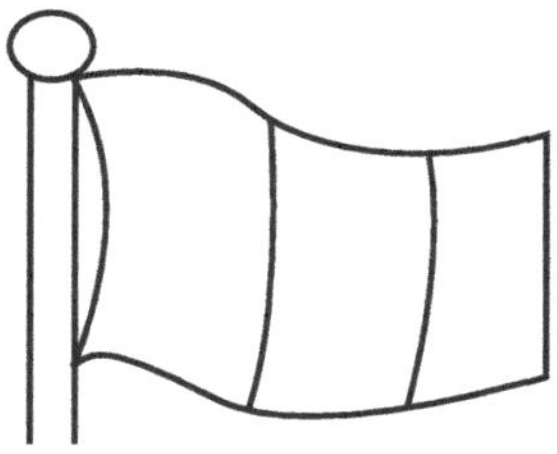 flag	 island

Use the picture clues to read these words starting with *i*.

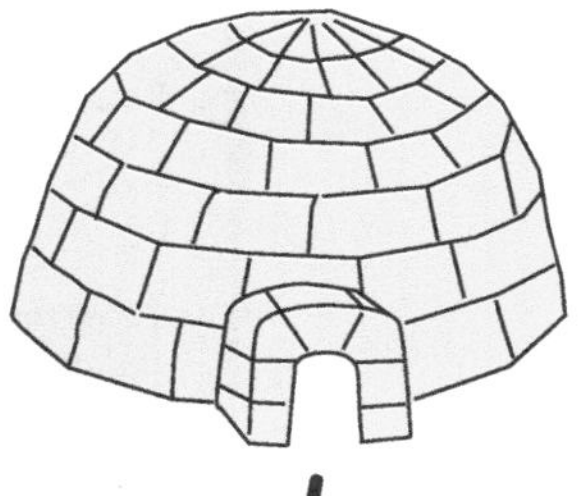

ink igloo iceblock ice cream

Nancy's Necklace

Practise saying the speech rhyme about *n*.

Nancy has a necklace
With nine and ninety beads.
Her necklace is so very nice
It is everything she needs.

Track the letter *N* between the lines. Start at the red dot.

Track

Trace the letter *n*. Start at the red dot.

Trace

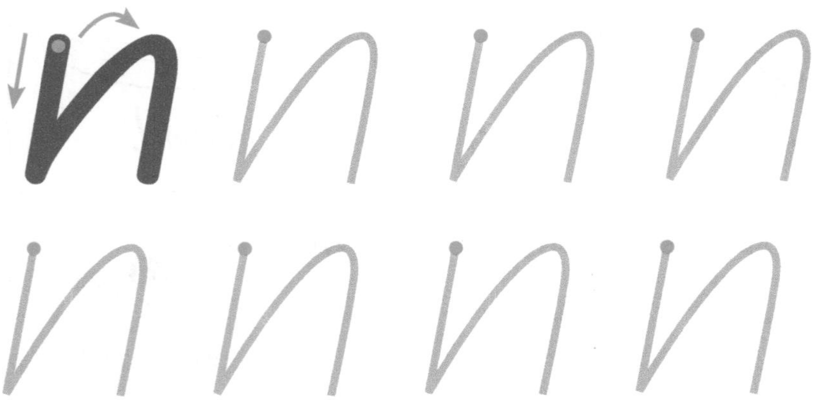

Practise saying out loud

'noises in the night n n n'

Colour the pictures in the row that begin with *n* sound.

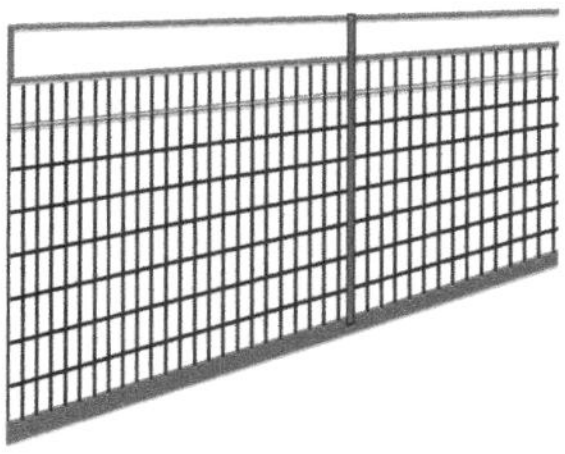 net	 fish	 necklace	 neck
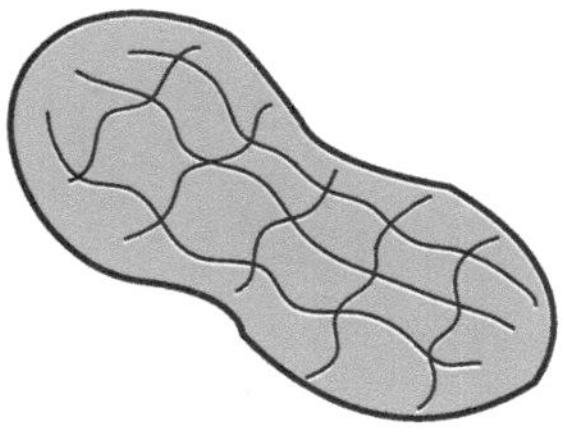 nut	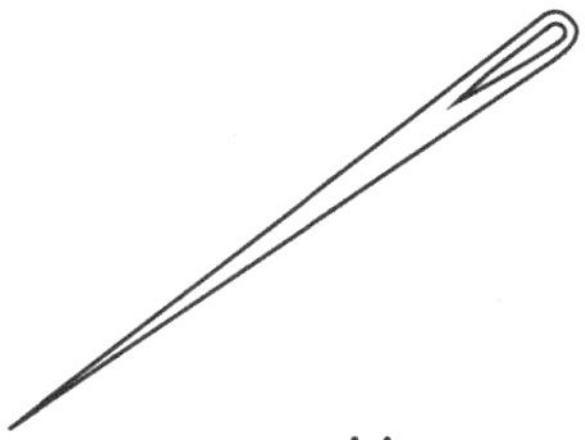 needle	 grapes	 nail
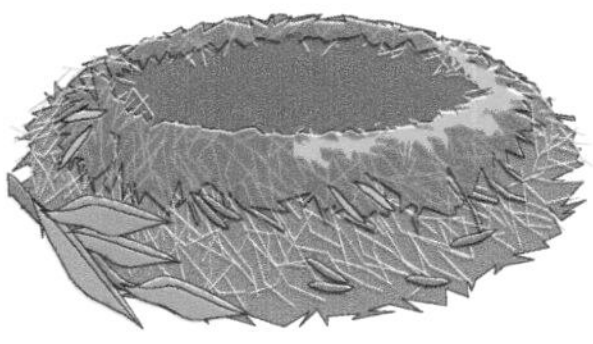 nest	 nurse	 nose	 ice cream
 nine	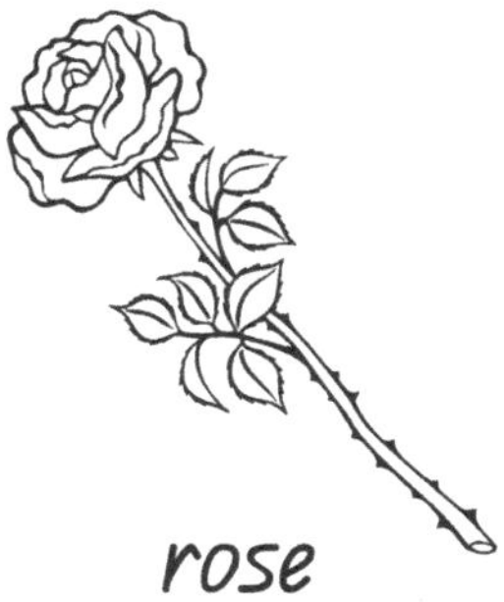 rose	 numbers	 newspaper

Use the picture clues to read these words starting with *n*.

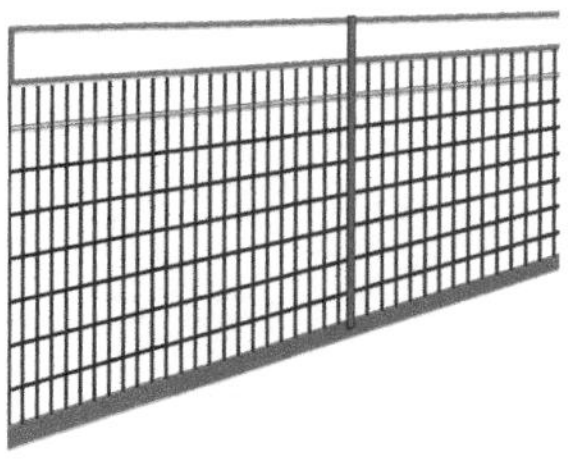

net

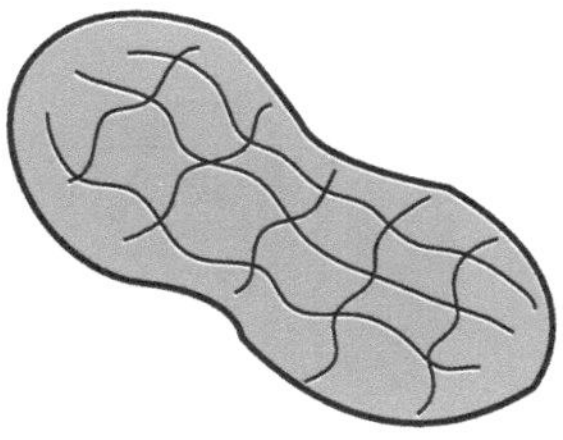

nut

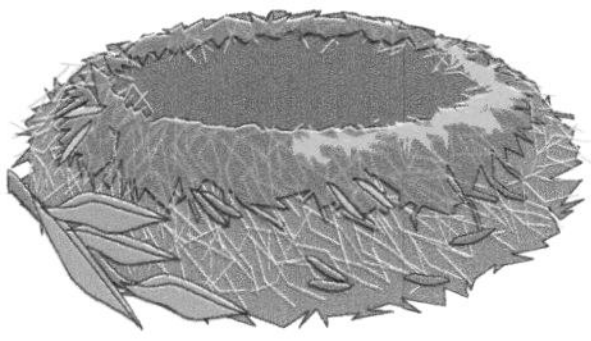

nest

nine

Eleven Elephants

Practise saying the speech rhyme about *e*.

Eleven hungry elephants
Eating lots of food.
Eleven happy elephants
In a better mood.

Track the letter *E* between the lines. Start at the red dot.

Track

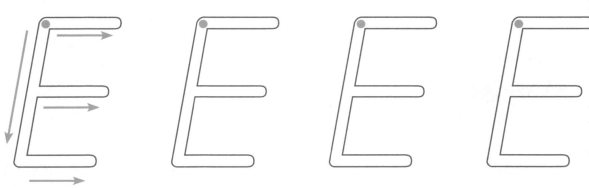

Trace the letter *e*. Start at the red dot.

Trace

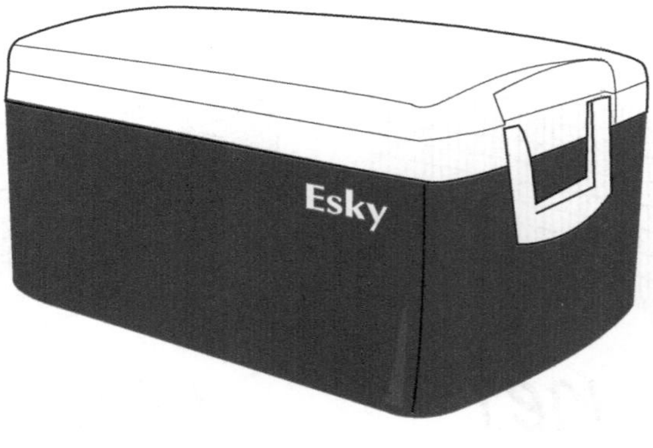

Practise saying out loud

'eggs in the esky e e e'

Colour the pictures in the row that begin with the short and long *e* sounds.

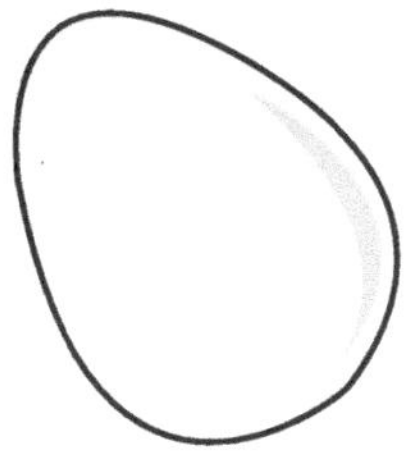 egg	 exit	 elephant	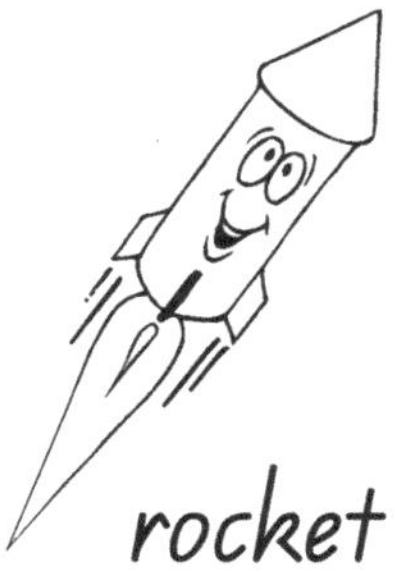 rocket
 elf	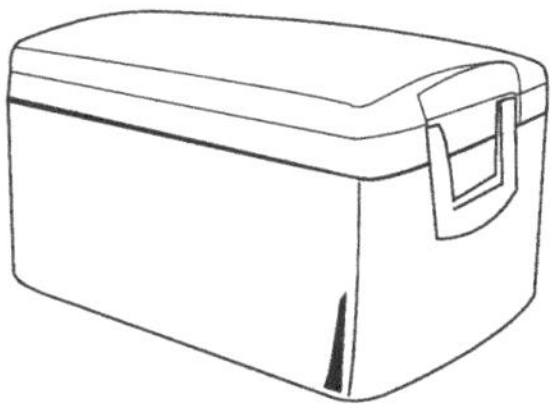 esky	 nail	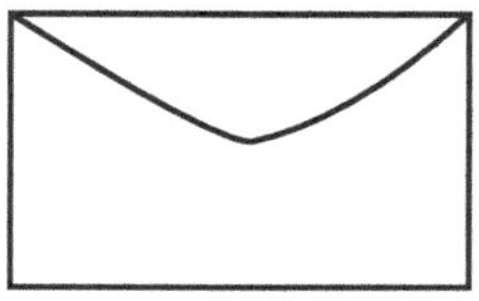 envelope
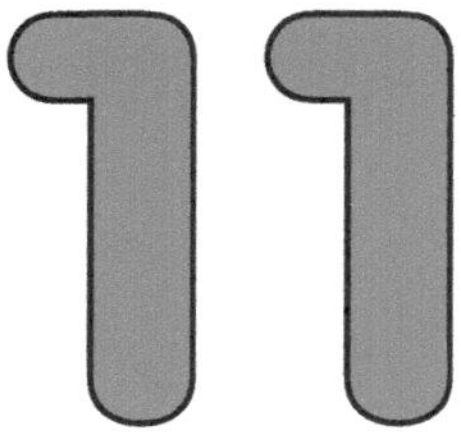 eleven	 rabbit	 empty	 elbow
 emu	 email	 eagle	 echidna

Use the picture clues to read these words starting with *e*.

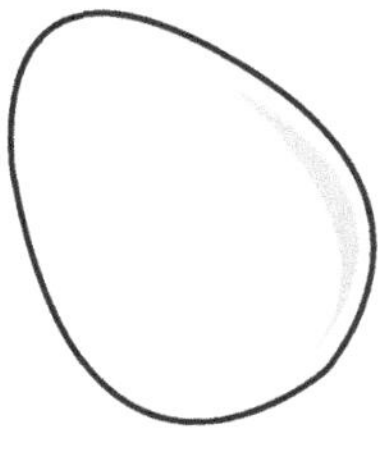
egg

elf

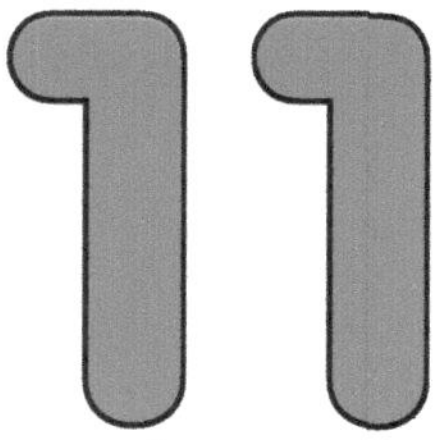
eleven

emu

Dripping

Practise saying the speech rhyme about *d*.

Drip, drip, drip, drip,
Dripping from the sky,
Down came the raindrops
Dripping from on high.

Track the letter *D* between the lines. Start at the red dot.

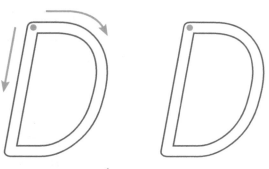

Track

D D D D

Trace the letter *d*. Start at the red dot.

Trace

d d d d
d d d

Practise saying out loud
'drainpipes dripping d d d'

Colour the pictures in the row that begin with *d* sound.

 dog	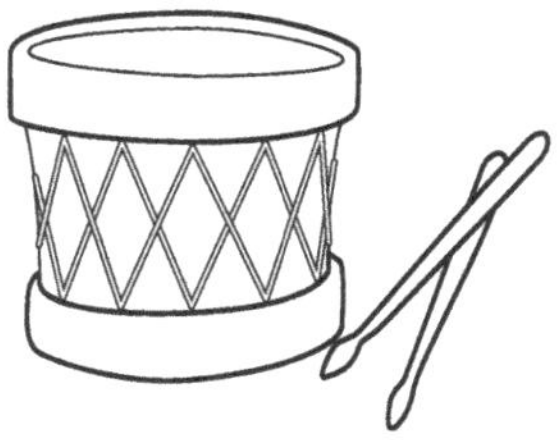 drum	 dinosaur	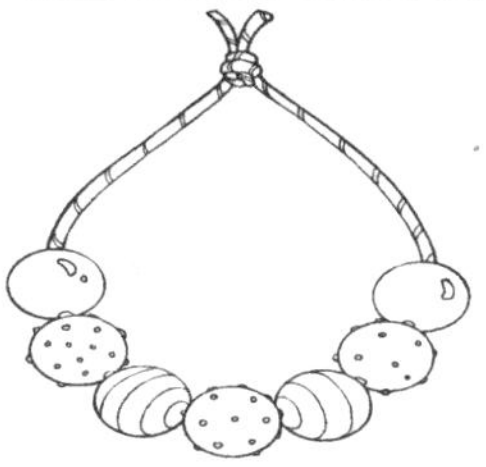 necklace
 doll	 dolphin	 elephant	 donkey
 duck	 nest	 daffodil	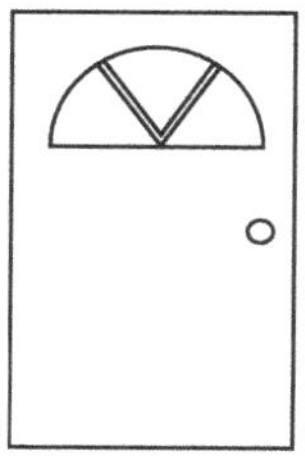 door
 dice	 dishes	 dress	 dig

Use the picture clues to read these words starting with *d*.

dog

doll

duck

dice

Hurry Up Harry

Practise saying the speech rhyme about *h*.

Hurry up Harry,
Hurry with your feet,
Your hungry horse is happy
When he has some hay to eat.

Track the letter *H* between the lines. Start at the red dot.

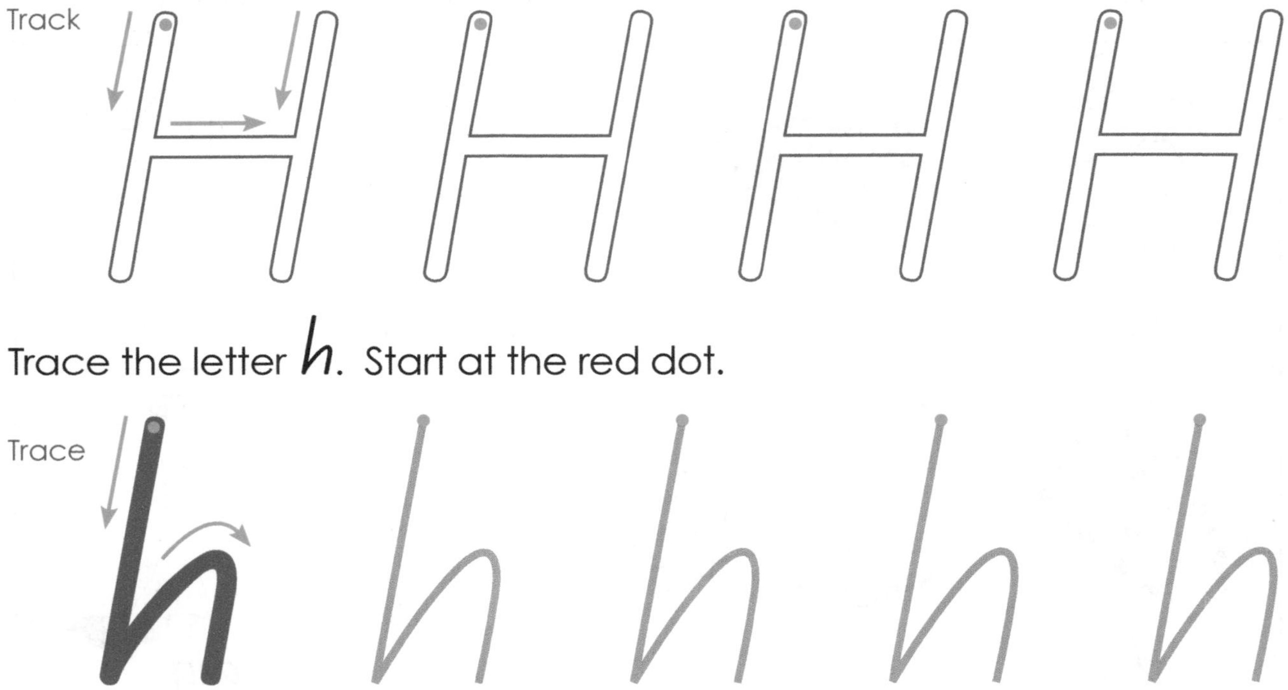

Trace the letter *h*. Start at the red dot.

Practise saying out loud
'hungry horses h h h'

Colour the pictures in the row that begin with *h* sound.

 hen	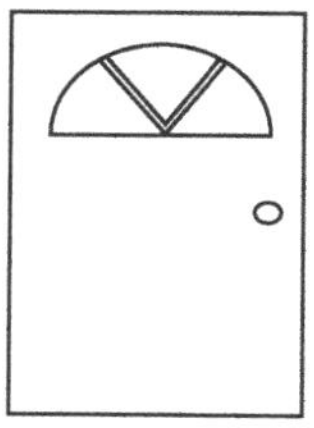 door	 horse	 hippopotamus
 hat	 heart	 five	 hamburger
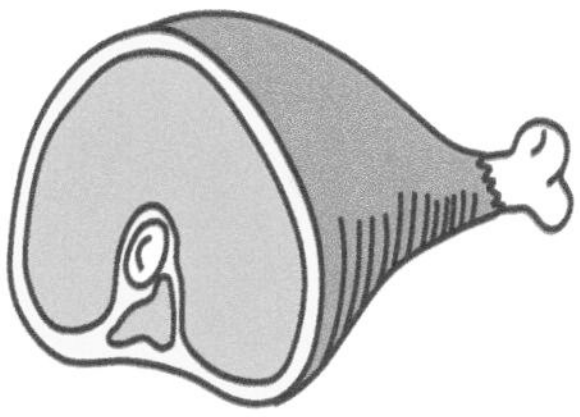 ham	 house	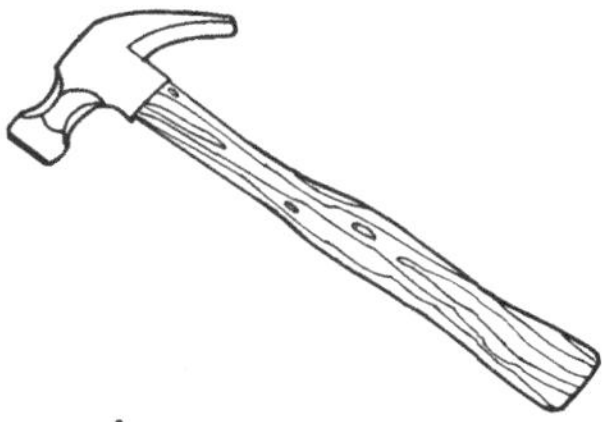 hammer	 hoop
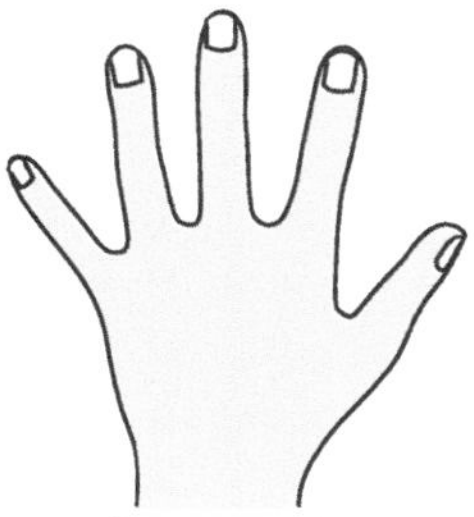 hand	 duck	 helicopter	 hose

Use the picture clues to read these words starting with *h*.

 hen	 hat	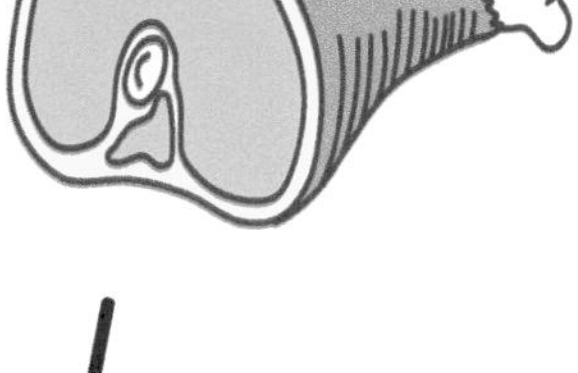 ham	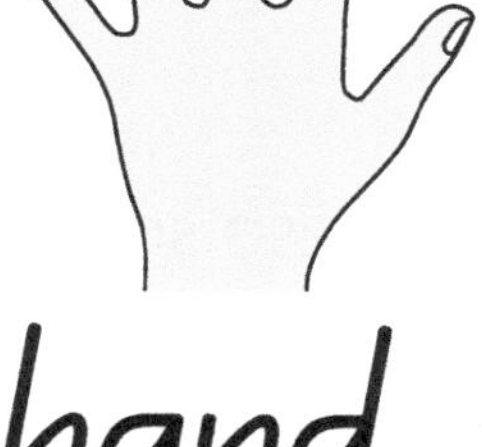 hand

Octopussy

Practise saying the speech rhyme about *o*.

I have octopussy friends
Who live down in the sea.
We play octopussy games
When they come to visit me.

Track the letter *O* between the lines. Start at the red dot.

Track

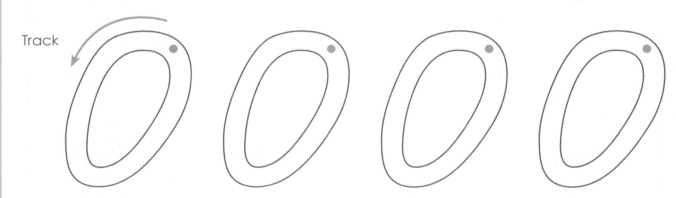

Trace the letter *O*. Start at the red dot.

Trace

Practise saying out loud

'Ozzie Octopus o o o'

Colour the pictures in the row that begin with the *o* sound.

 ox	 octopus	 hen	 ostrich
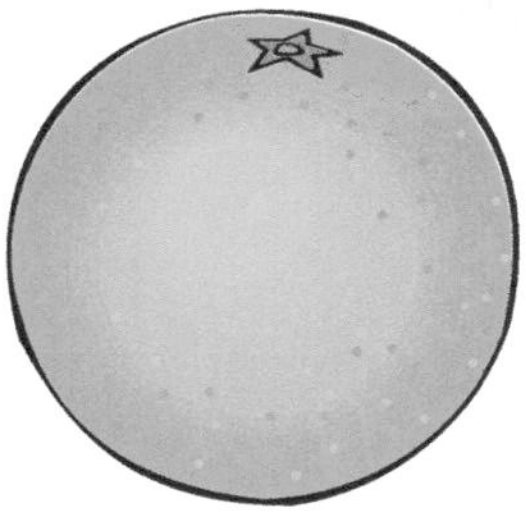 orange	 dinosaur	 Opera House	 Olympic rings
 orange	 orang-outang	 tree	

Use the picture clues to read these words starting with *o*.

ox

orange

ostrich

Opera House

Ladybird

Practise saying the speech rhyme about *l*.

Ladybird, ladybird,
On a leafy tree.
Fly away ladybird,
Fly here to me.

Track the letter *L* between the lines. Start at the red dot.

Track

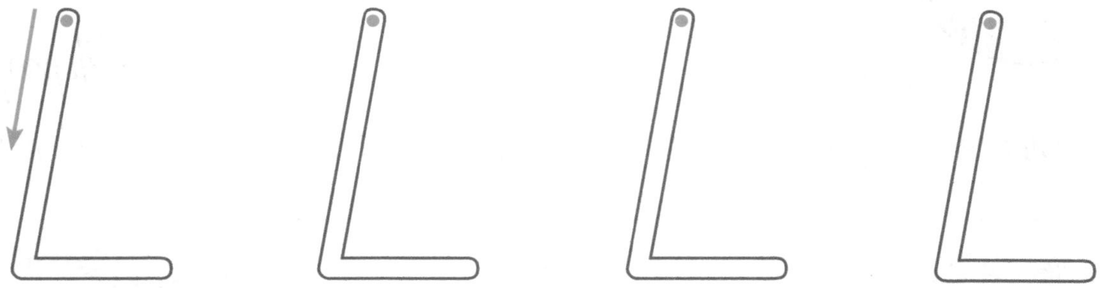

Trace the letter *l*. Start at the red dot.

Trace

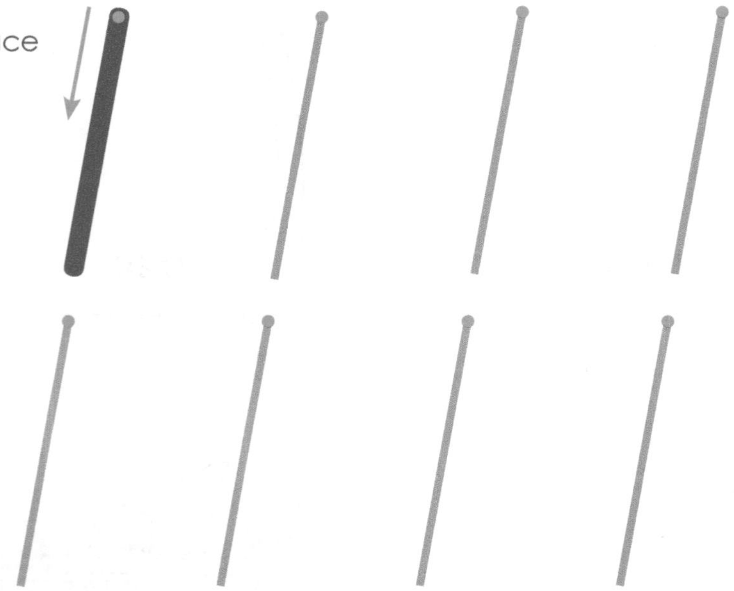

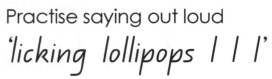

Practise saying out loud
'licking lollipops l l l'

Colour the pictures in the row that begin with *l* sound.

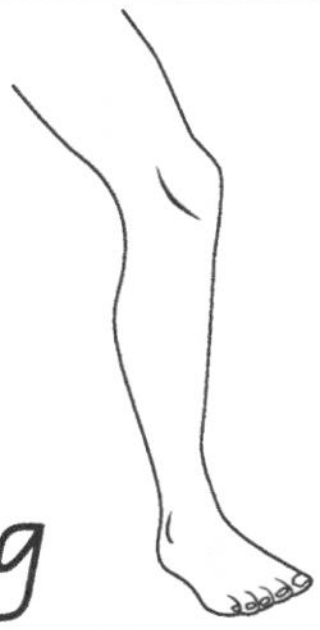 leg	 ladybird	 hammer	 leaf
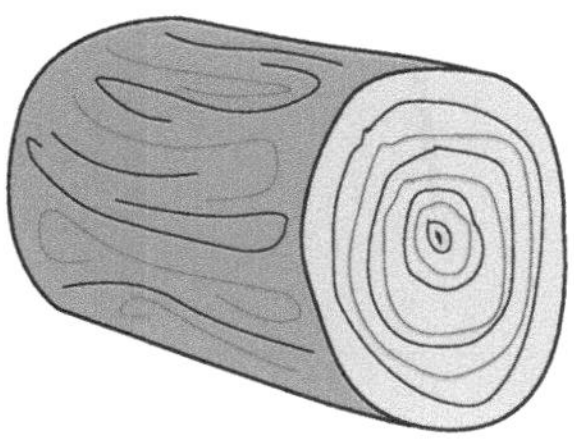 log	 lizard	 lion	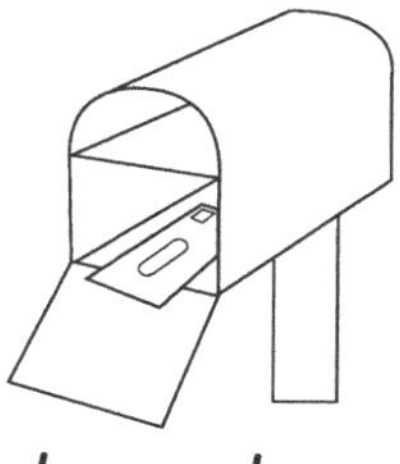 letterbox
 lips	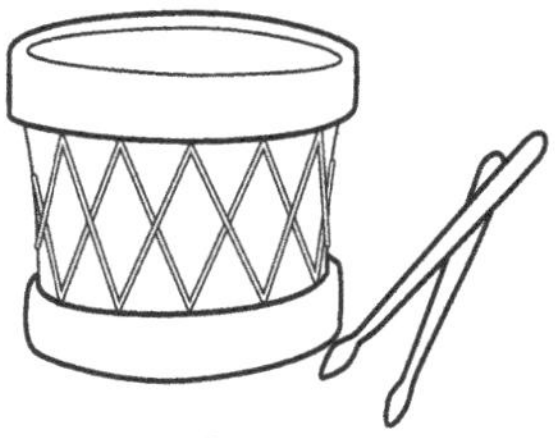 drum	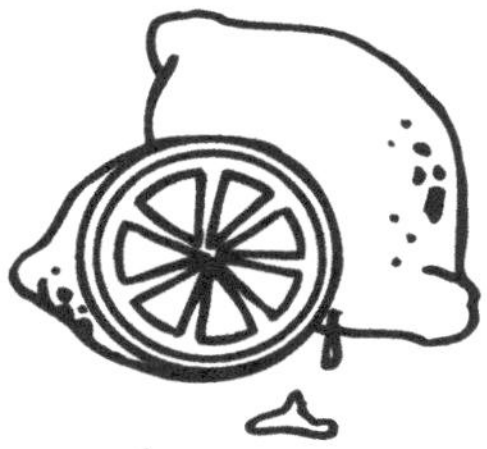 lemon	 lamb
 lollipop	 letter	 sun	 ladder

Use the picture clues to read these words starting with *l*.

 leg	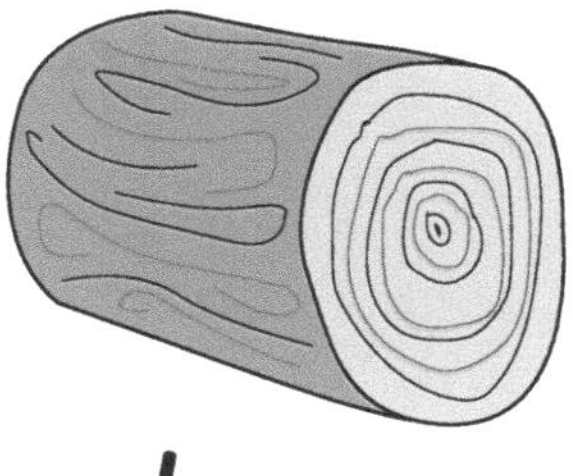 log	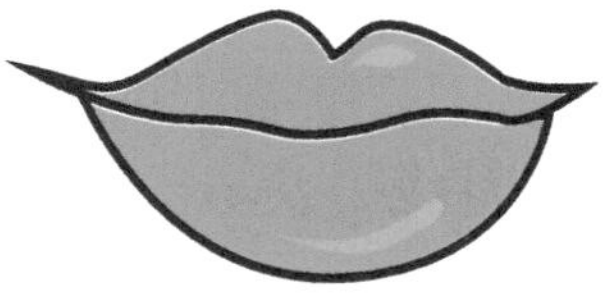 lips	 lollipops

Beginning Sounds

Circle the letter that makes the beginning sound to match each picture.

d r i

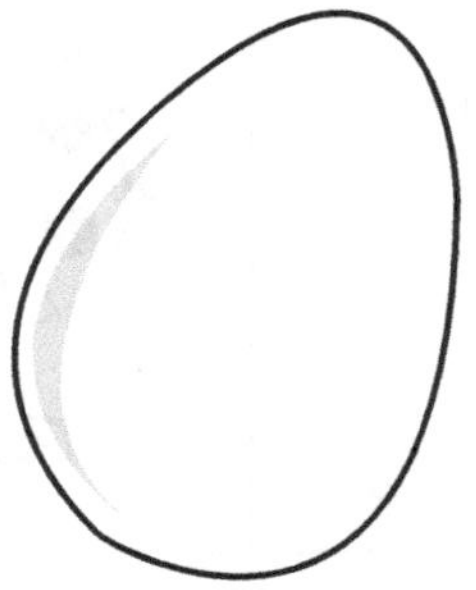

n e l

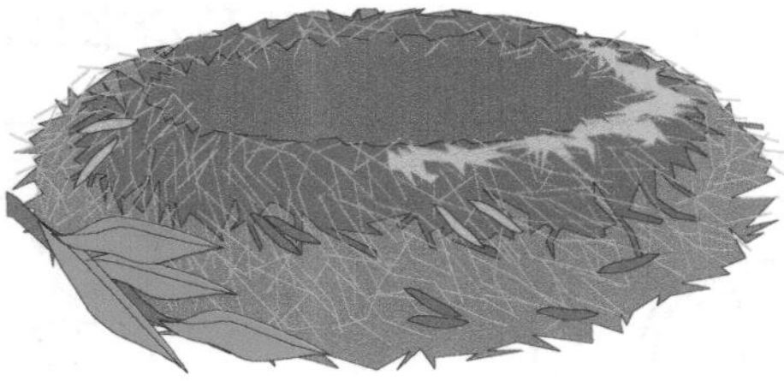

n o h

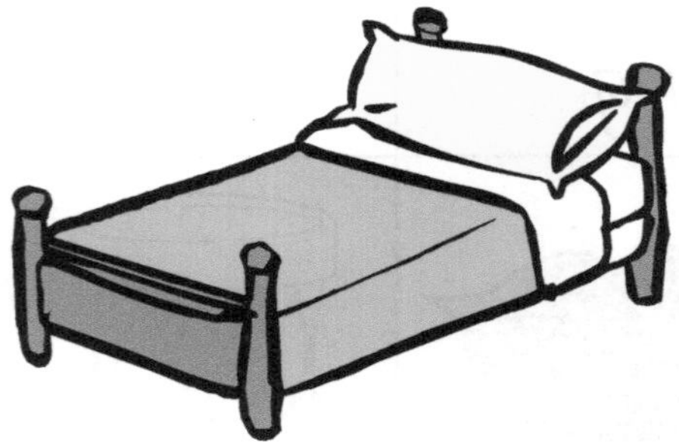

r b g

t s f

r d c

Read

a red bed

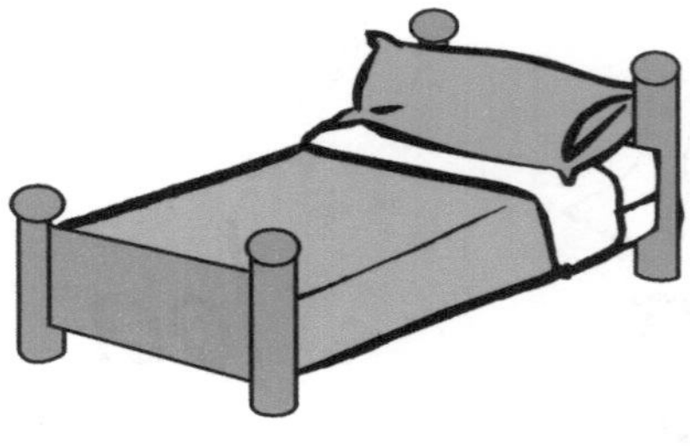

Missing Letters

Write the missing letters.

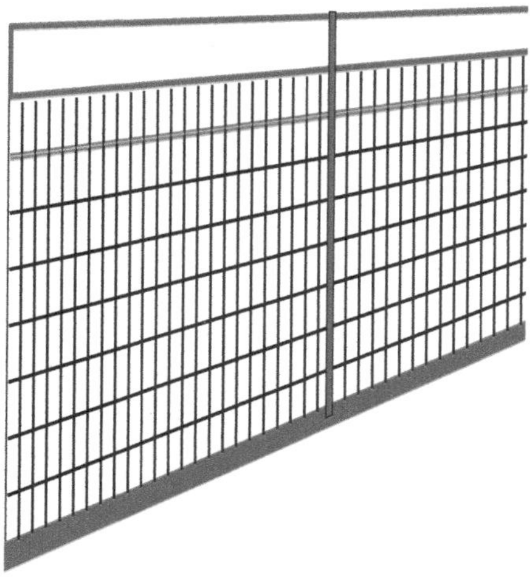

___ et   bi___   do___

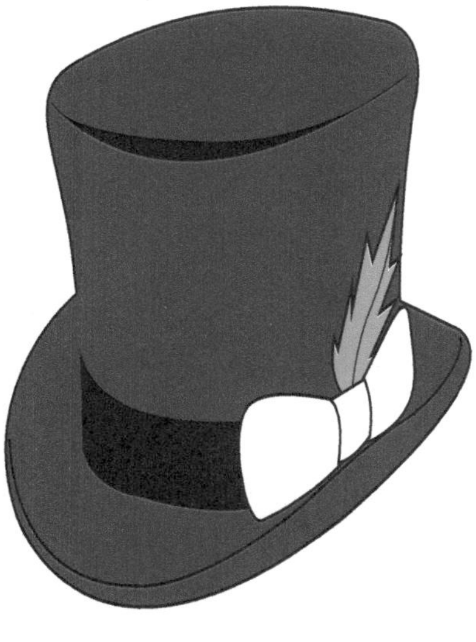

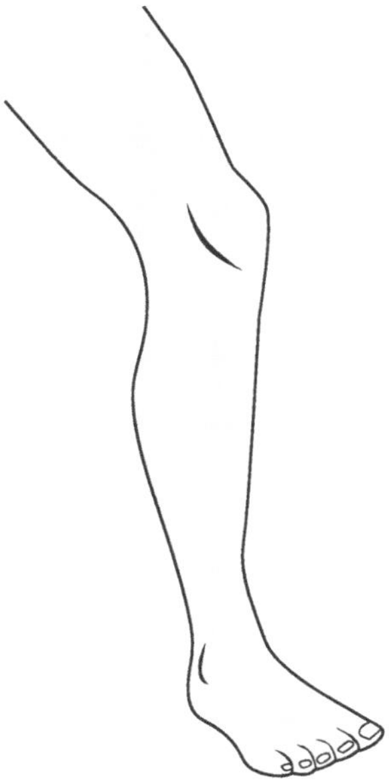

ha___   le___   be___

Percy Pig

Practise saying the speech rhyme about *p*.

Percy is a perfect pig,
A present from my mummy.
When I have some coins to spare
I put them in his tummy.

Track the letter *P* between the lines. Start at the red dot.

Track

Trace the letter *p*. Start at the red dot.

Trace

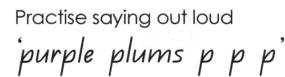

Practise saying out loud

'purple plums p p p'

Colour the pictures in the row that begin with *p* sound.

 pig	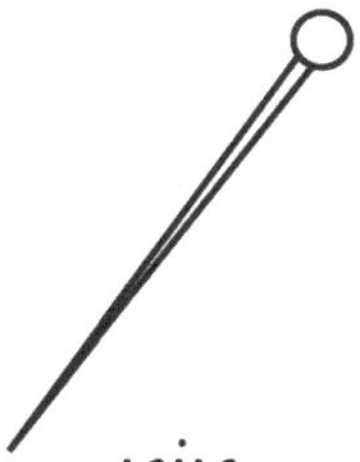 pin	 plane	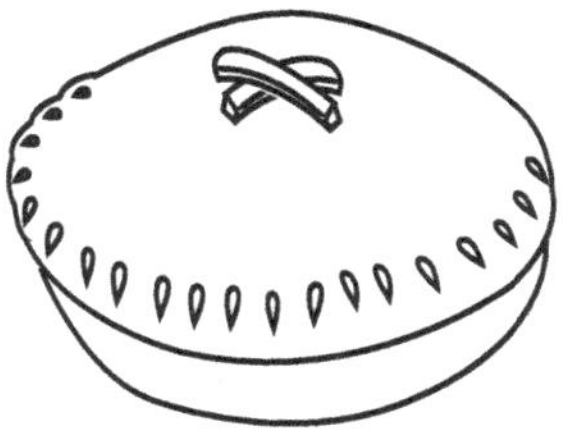 pie
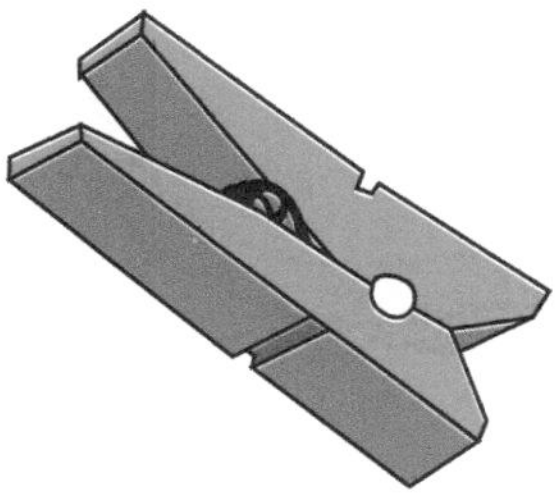 peg	 pineapple	 plum	 present
 pup	 pear	 penguin	 parachute
 pen	 possum	 pelican	 platypus

Use the picture clues to read these words starting with *p*.

pig

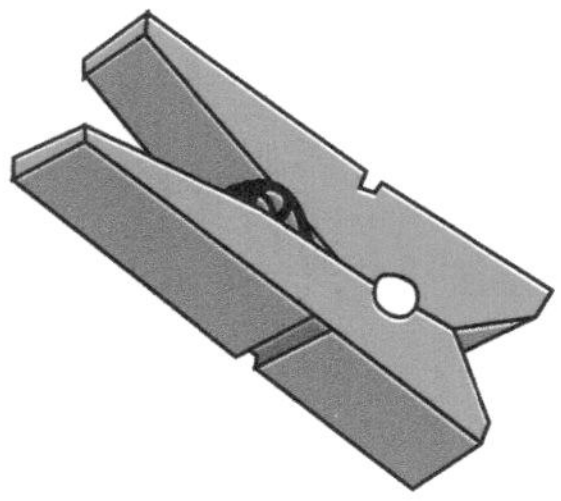
peg

pup

pen

Watermelon

Practise saying the speech rhyme about *w*.

Watermelon, watermelon,
Juicy, ripe and sweet,
I eat it with my friends at school.
Wow - a yummy treat!

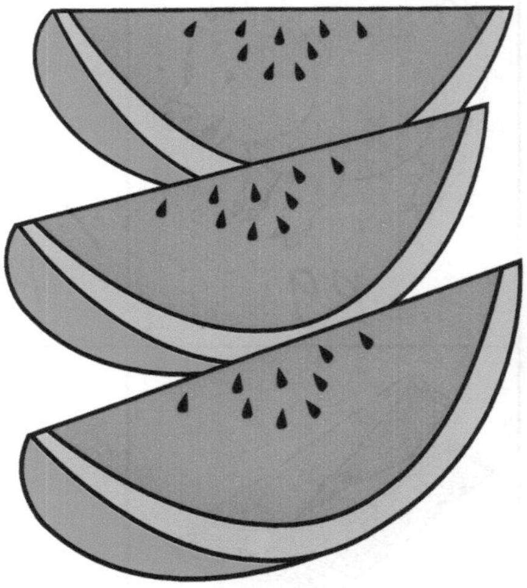

Track the letter W between the lines. Start at the red dot.

Track

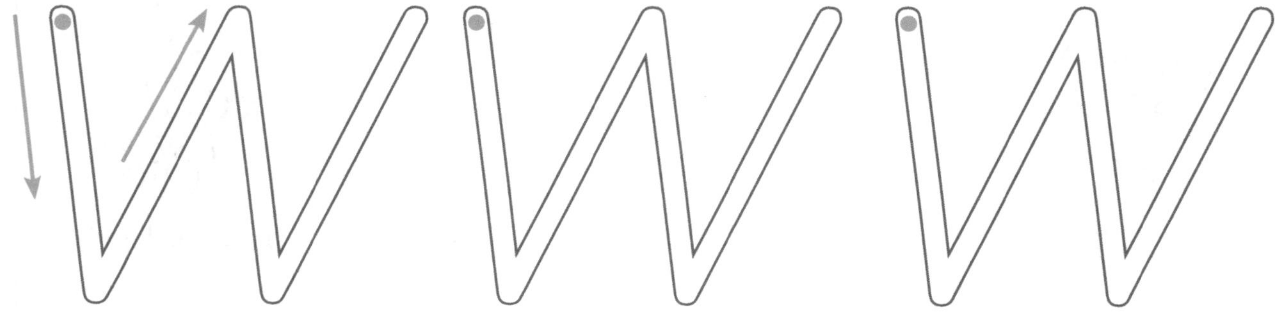

Trace the letter *w*. Start at the red dot.

Trace

Practise saying out loud

'wallabies wobbling w w w'

Colour the pictures in the row that begin with *w* sound.

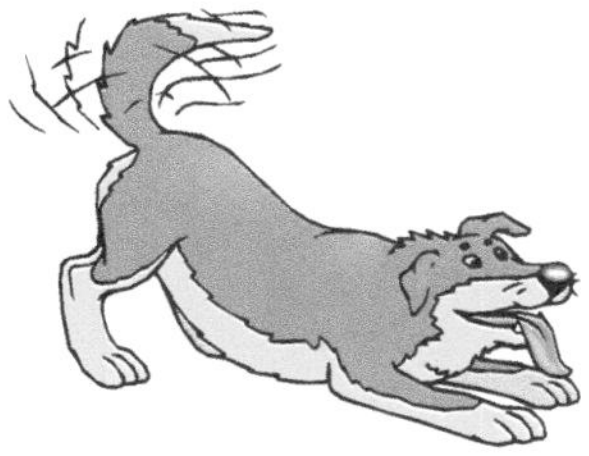 wag	 watermelon	 windmill	 dolphin
 wig	 worm	 wombat	 wasp
 web	 horse	 wave	 wink
 wax	 rainbow	 watch	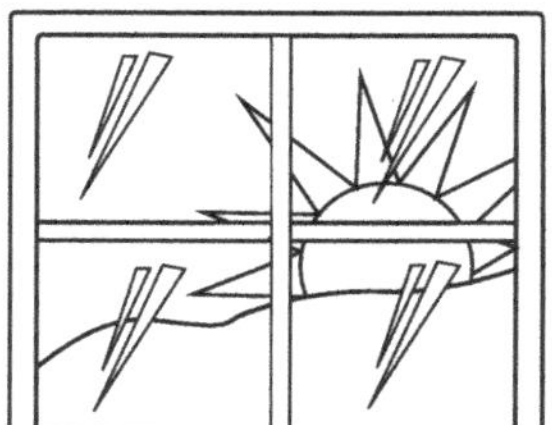 window

Use the picture clues to read these words starting with *w*.

wag

wig

web

wax

Kicks

Practise saying the speech rhyme about *k*.

Kick with your left foot,
Kick with your right,
Kick that brown ball
Out of sight.

Track the letter K between the lines. Start at the red dot.

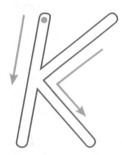

Track

K K K K

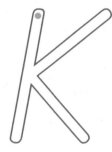

Trace the letter *k*. Start at the red dot.

Trace

k k k k k

k k k

Practise saying out loud

'kangaroos kicking k k k'

Colour the pictures in the row that begin with *k* sound.

 kid	 kettle	 keys	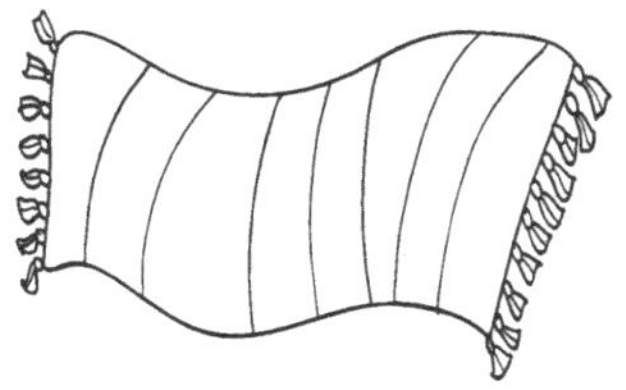 mat
 kick	 kennel	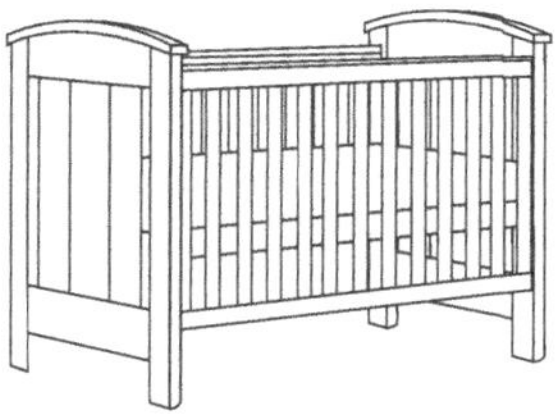 cot	 keyboard
 king	 bus	 kangaroo	 kite
 kitten	 kookaburra	 lollipop	 koala

Use the picture clues to read these words starting with *k*.

kid

kick

king

kitten

Jumping

Practise saying the speech rhyme about *j*.

Jump, jump, jump!
Jump up high.
Jump in the air,
Touch the sky.

Track the letter *J* between the lines. Start at the red dot.

Track

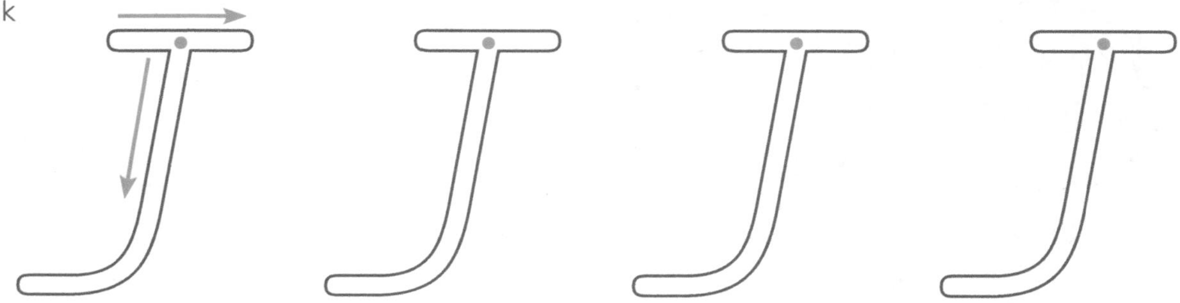

Trace the letter *j*. Start at the red dot.

Trace

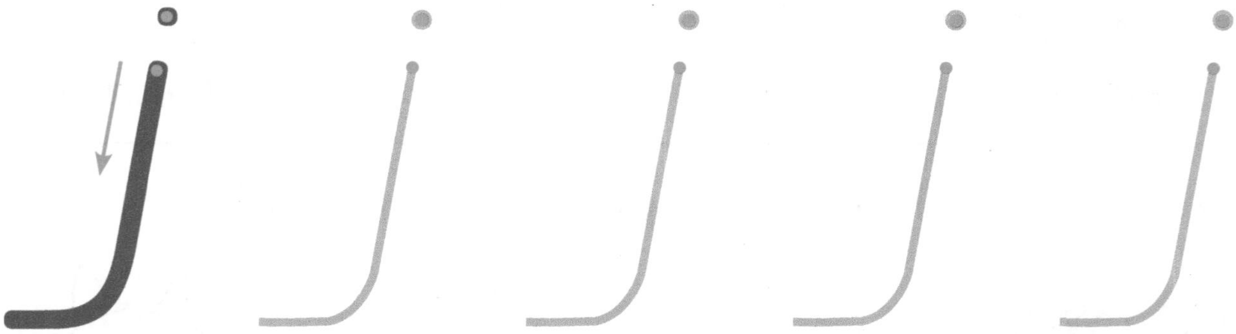

Practise saying out loud

'jumping jellybeans j j j'

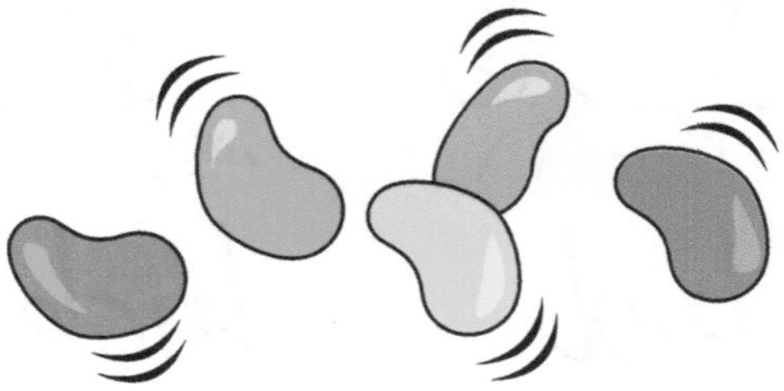

Colour the pictures in the row that begin with *j* sound.

 jam	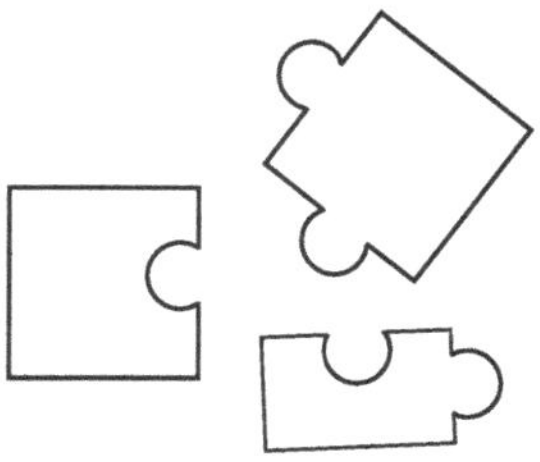 jigsaw	 heart	 juice
 jug	 juggling	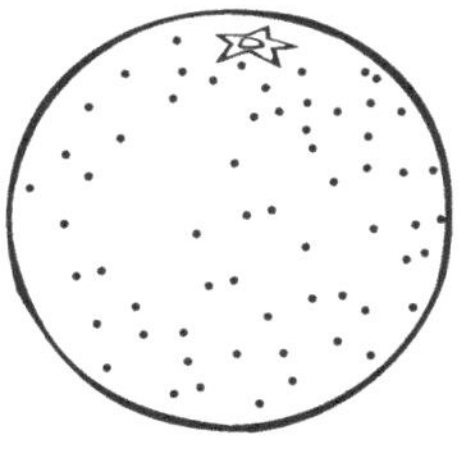 orange	 jeep
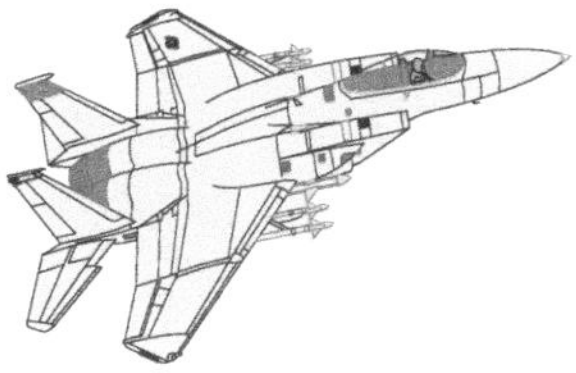 jet	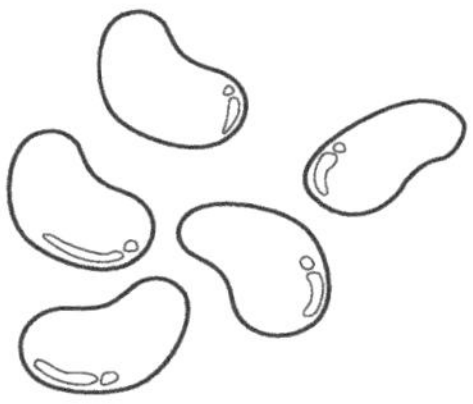 jellybeans	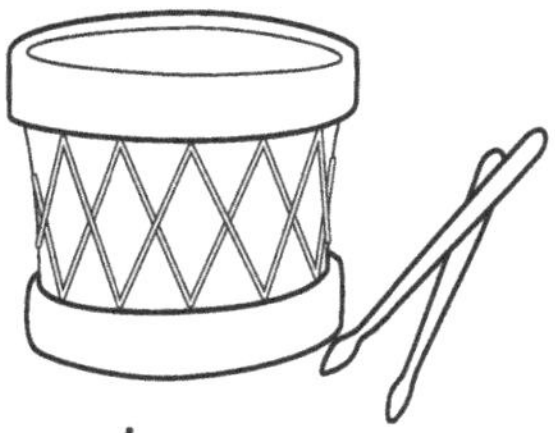 drum	 Jack-in-the-box
 jelly	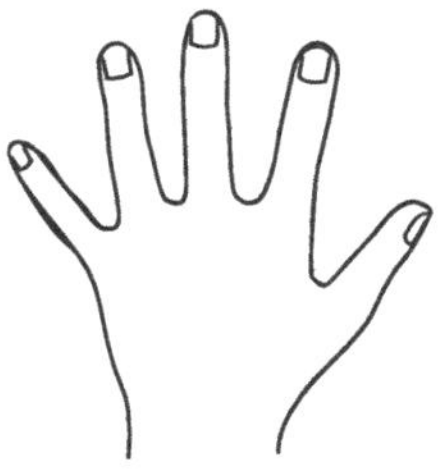 hand	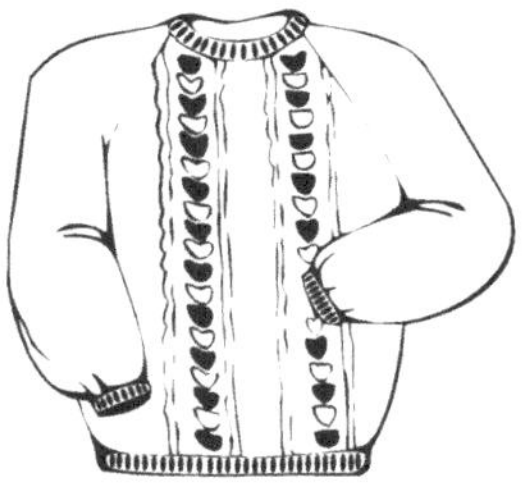 jumper	 jacket

Use the picture clues to read these words starting with *j*.

jam

jug

jet

jelly

Quack Quack

Practise saying the speech rhyme about *q*.

Here come the quiet ducks,
Quack, quack, quack.
Here come the noisy ones,
QUACK! QUACK! QUACK!

Track the letter *Q* between the lines. Start at the red dot.

Track

Trace the letter *q*. Start at the red dot.

Trace

Practise saying out loud

Queen *question mark* *quarter*

My Umbrella

Practise saying the speech rhyme about *u*.

Up went my umbrella
One rainy, rainy day.
I held it very tightly
But the wind blew it away!

Track the letter *u* between the lines. Start at the red dot.

Track

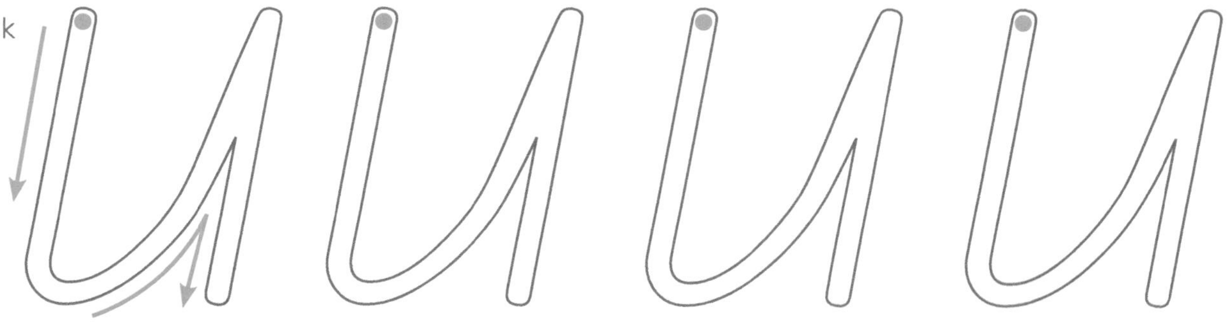

Trace the letter *u*. Start at the red dot.

Trace

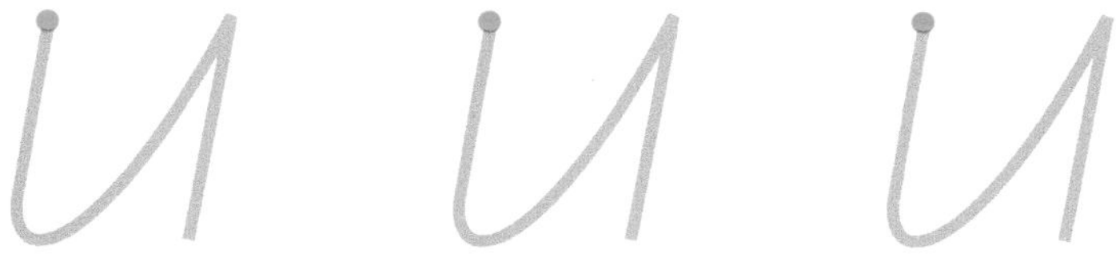

Practise saying out loud

up *umbrella* *upset*

Vera

Practise saying the speech rhyme about *v*.

Vera plays the violin
Very, very well.
She does a lot of practice,
Everyone can tell.

Track the letter V between the lines. Start at the red dot.

Track

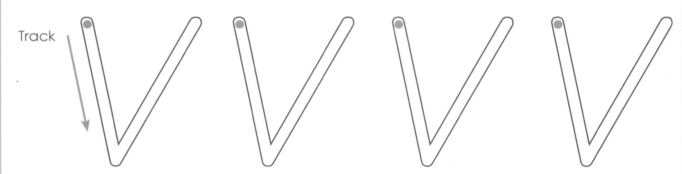

Trace the letter *v*. Start at the red dot.

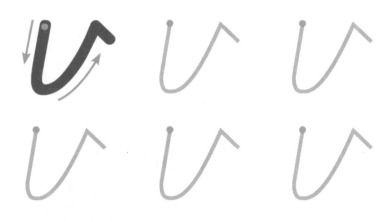

Trace

Practise saying out loud

'very hot volcanoes v v v'

Colour the pictures in the row that begin with v sound.

van

vase

frog

violets

vet

Valentine

dice

vegetables

volcano

vacuum cleaner

ram

violin

Use the picture clues to read these words starting with v.

van

volcano

Vet

Foxes

Practise saying the speech rhyme about **x**.

How many foxes live in boxes?
Five or six, five or six?
Do we need to X-ray them?
What a fix, what a fix!

Trace the letter X. Start at the red dot.

Trace

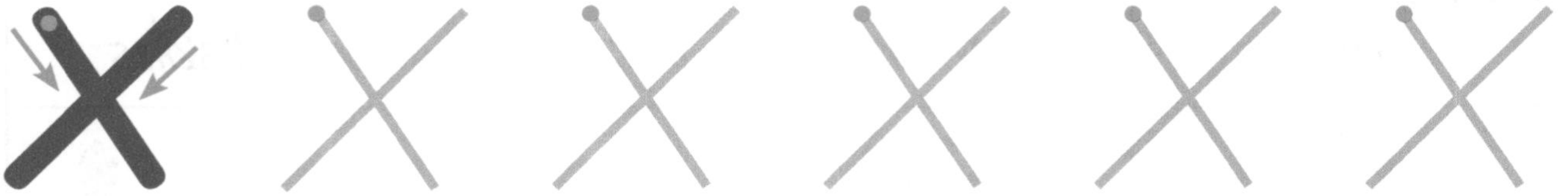

Practise saying out loud

'six foxes in six boxes x x x'

Use the picture clues to read these words starting or ending with **x**.

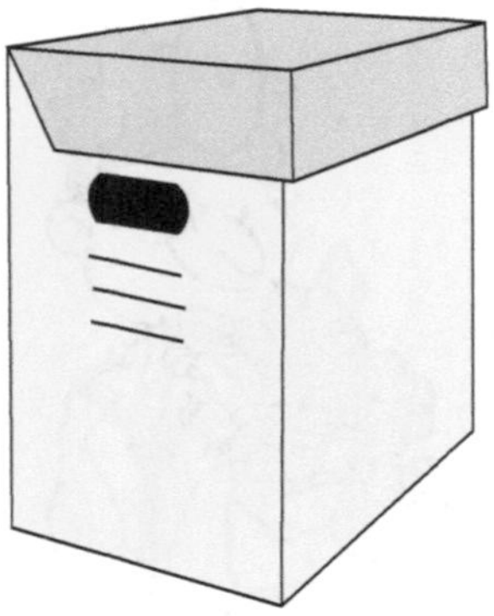

box

fox

six

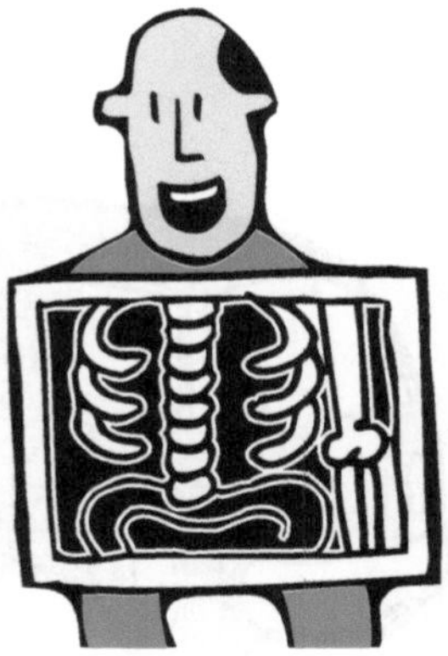

X-ray

Yo Yo

Practise saying the speech rhyme about *y*.

I have a yellow yo yo,
Up and down it goes,
Up on my fingers
And down to my toes.

Trace the letter *y*. Start at the red dot.

Trace

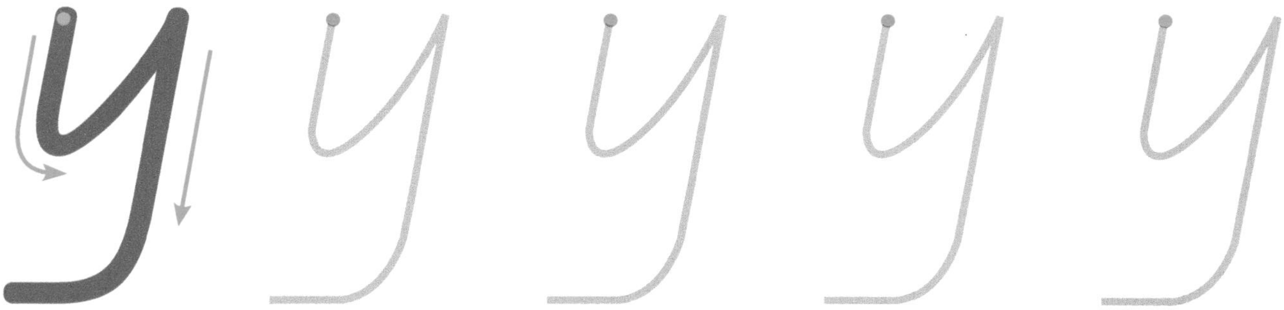

Practise saying out loud

'yellow yabbies y y y'

Use the picture clues to read these words starting or ending with *y*.

yo yo *yellow* *yabby*

Zig Zag

Practise saying the speech rhyme about **z**.

Zebras can go zig zag
On zebra crossings too,
Do people need to zip across
Like the zebras do?

Trace the letter **z**. Start at the red dot.

Trace

Practise saying out loud

'zebras zipping z z z'

Use the picture clues to read these words starting with **z**.

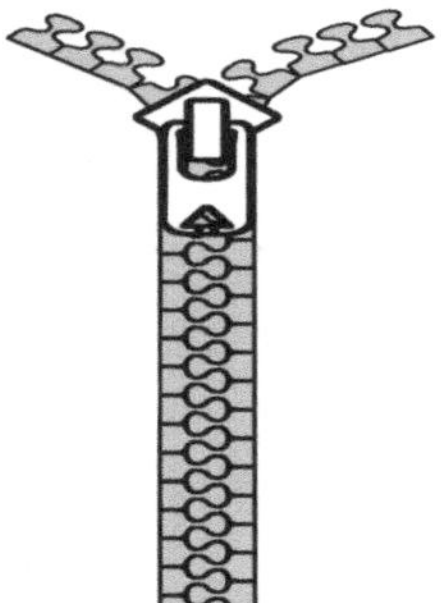

zoo *zipper* *zero*

Colour the pictures in the row that begin with the **short and long** *u* sounds.

umbrella

umpire

ute

unicorn

Colour the pictures in the row that begin or end with *x* sound.

six

box

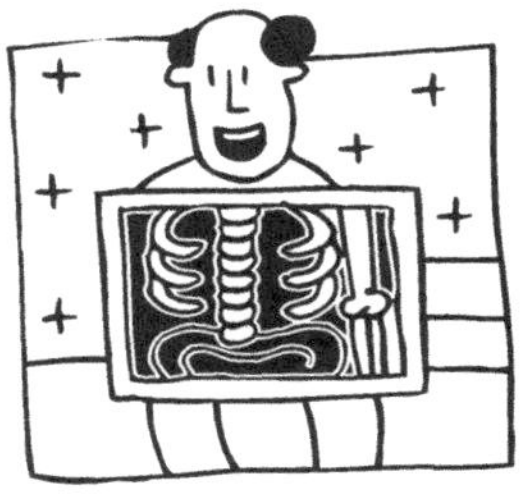

x-ray

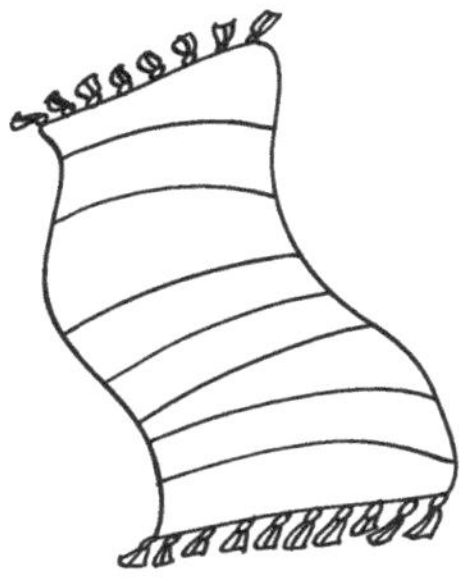

mat

Colour the pictures in the row that begin with *y* sound.

yo yo

yacht

ant

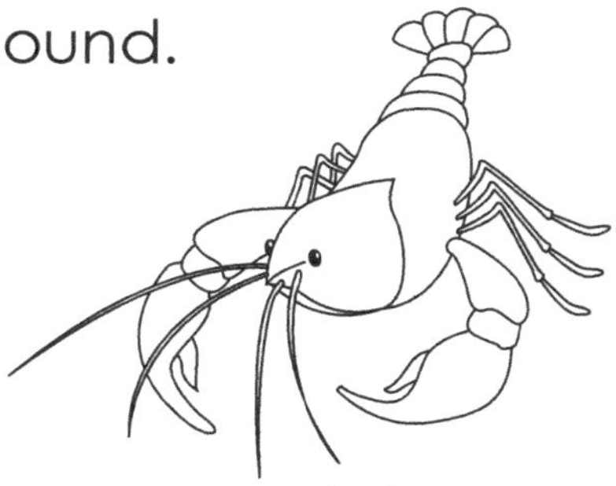

yabby

Colour the pictures in the row that begin with *z* sound.

zebra

dice

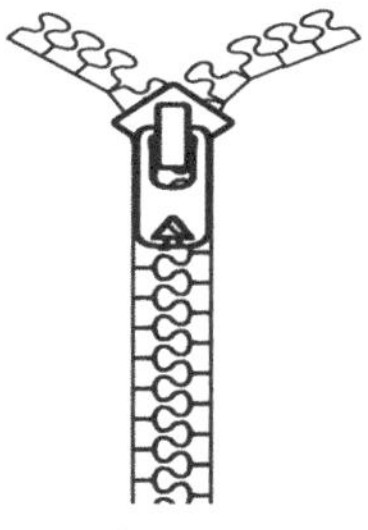

zipper

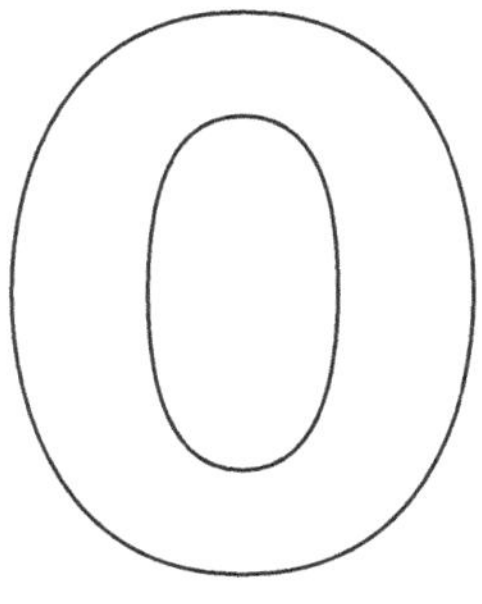

zero

Beginning Sounds

Circle the letter that makes the beginning sound to match each picture.

p e z

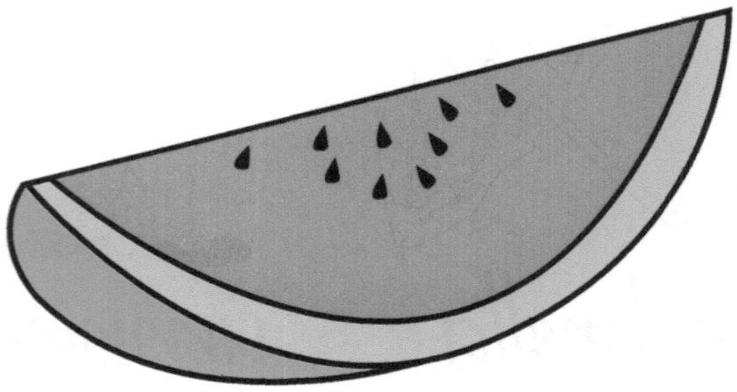

x a w

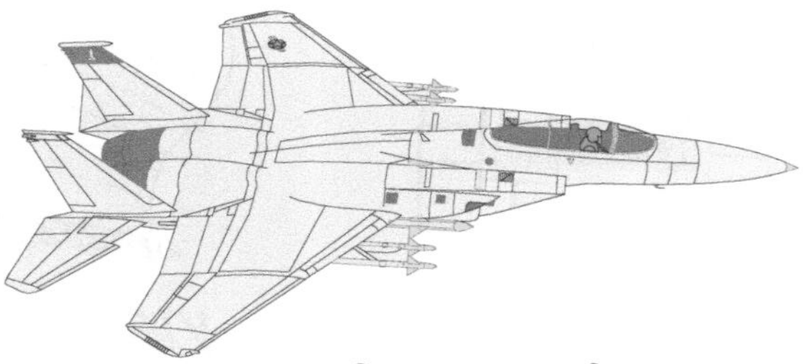

j h d

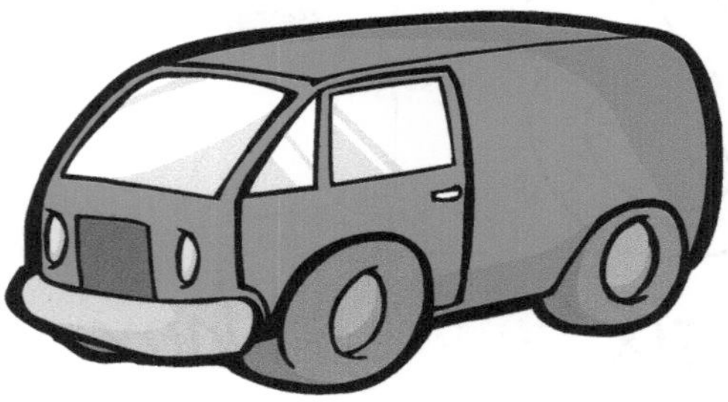

v p y

j g y

i q n

Read

a pet hen

Missing Letters

Write the missing letters.

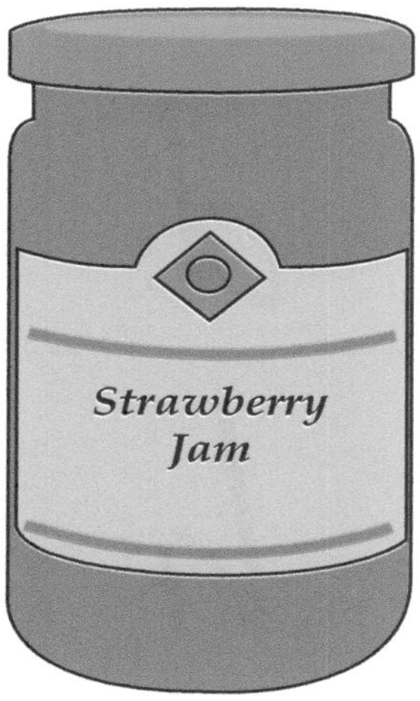

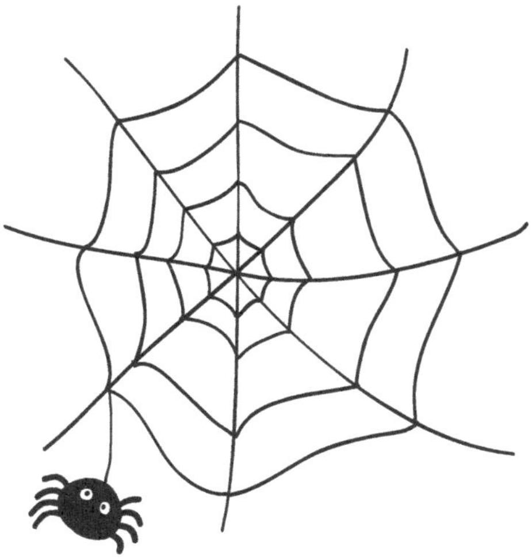

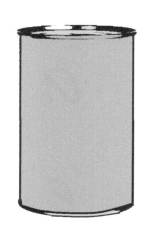

j ___ m   w ___ b   t ___ n

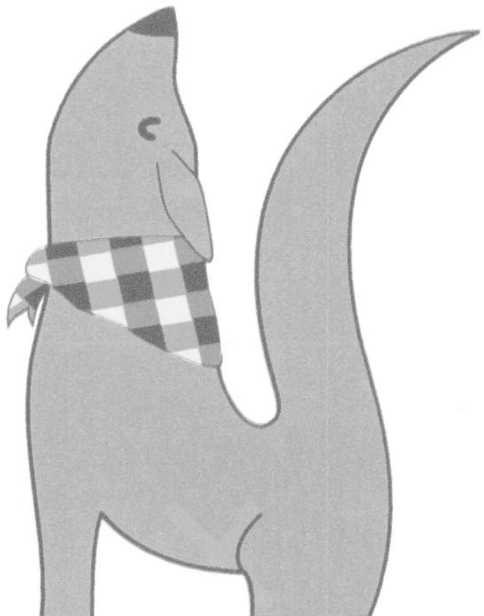

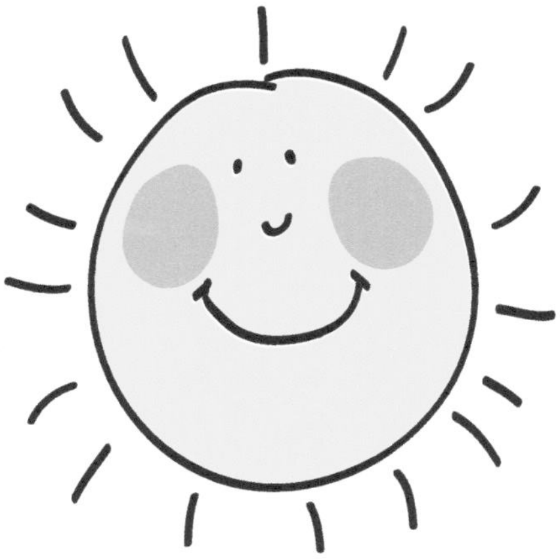

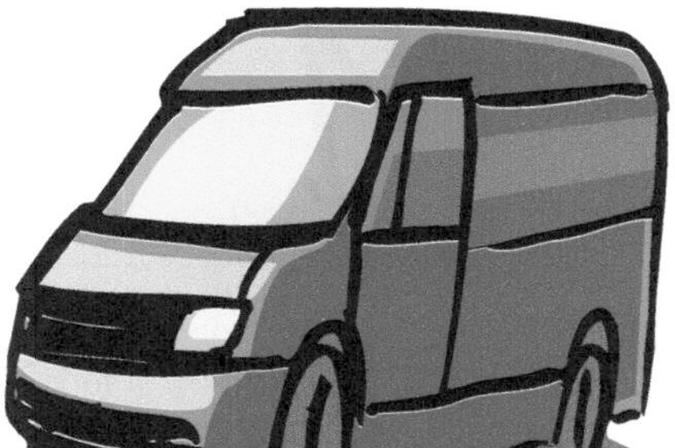

d ___ g   s ___ n   v ___ n

Assessment Task

Oral assessment task for individual articulation of letters and their initial sounds.

a	b	c	d
e	f	g	h
i	j	k	l
m	n	o	p
q	r	s	t
u	v	w	x
y	z		

Score: /26

I can read!

Introduce different sound for *a* in this context.

a red hat 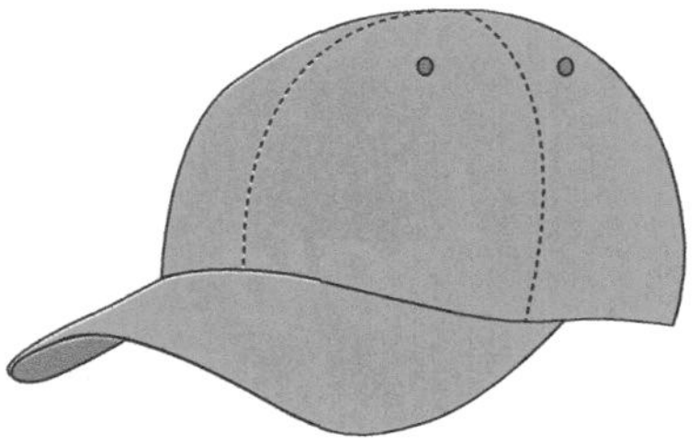

a big bus

a fat pup 

 a red dot

 a big pig

I can run.

I can hop.

I can pat a dog.

I can go in a big jet.

I can go in a
big red bus.

I can spell!

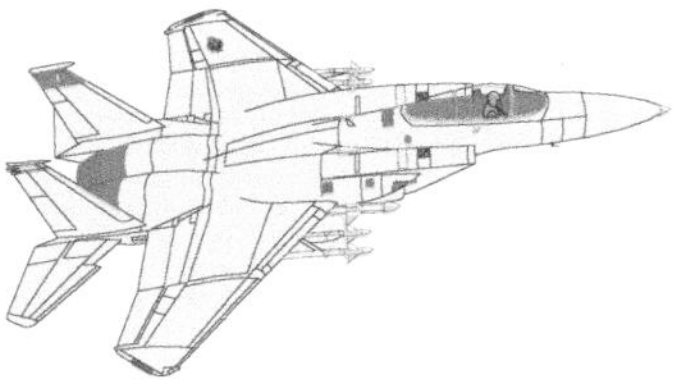

Ten Point Checklist

The student can ....

- Articulate initial sounds in a speech rhyme.
- Trace and colour upper and lower case letter shapes.
- Articulate sounds correctly in a phonic jingle.
- Identify pictures and matching words beginning with a given letter/sound.
- Use picture clues for word/picture matching.
- Write the missing initial sounds in a word to match a picture.
- Write the missing middle sound in a word to match a picture.
- Write the missing end sound in a word to match a picture.
- Recognise each letter of the alphabet and articulate its initial sound.
- Read phrases and short sentences mainly using simple CVC words.